# Sullivan:

# Putting the Tri in Triumph

Cover photograps by Photography by Corinna

Layout and Design by Andy Grachuk © 2013
www.JingotheCat.com

"When I look into your eyes. It's like watching the night sky. Or a beautiful sunrise. Well there's so much they hold. And just like them old stars, I see that you've come so far. To be right where you are. How old is your soul? I won't give up on us. Even if the skies get rough. I'm giving you all my love. I'm still looking up." (Jason Mraz, "I Won't Give Up")

"He is your friend, your partner, your defender, your dog. You are his life, his love, his leader. He will be yours, faithful and true, to the last beat of his heart. You owe it to him to be worthy of such devotion."

Sullivan, you are my hero, inspiration and kindred friend. We never have, nor will, give up on each other. Ever. I love you.

Dear Someone, Anyone...                                         March 5, 2005

    Been living along this threatening Tennessee Interstate Road for a month or two now. A large woman in a sheer housedress abruptly dropped Ma, my five siblings, and me off one eventful night in two cramped plastic milk crates. Dumped right around the Exit 17 split. Ain't got no name and don't know my age, though I reckon I'm four or five months old by now. Am coming to know the many winds and turns of Interstate 40 pretty well, guess I could call it home.

    We spend our long, lonely days scavenging for food, trying to keep cool in shady spots, and not get seen by them creepy County Animal Control folks. They vigorously roam 40 looking for us strays. Hear the unlucky waifs get taken to a really scary, dark place and ain't never seen or heard from again. Ma's taught us to be extra careful and always have our wits.

    Tennessee southern sun is fiery hot, and them pavement cinders scorch our paw pads. We burrow at night under thistle, brush and hay, huddling close to keep safe and not draw attention. We take short shifts staying up in the night to keep watch over us all. Food and water are tough to come by. Motorcycle riders and cement truck drivers are kind folks and often throw assorted diner scraps, bones or even Slim Jim logs our way. Them little morsels satisfy our aching bellies a little, but never leave us full after sharing 7 ways.

    Just don't know how much longer we can keep on keepin' on. There's gotta be a better life for us; maybe a caring and helping soul to take us in? Ma's told us pups that in the end, only kindness matters. I wanna believe, but we're all so hot, tired, weak and hungry. Ain't no life for four-leggeds like us, especially Ma. We deserve a chance. Don't we?

    Look! A cement truck's slowing and pulling to the shoulder! He's picking us up one by one. Gonna take us somewhere. Says we're going to Miss Emily Dillman's. Told she's a kind lady who watches over strays like us. My faith is fading fast, but I still cling to some lingering hope just the same.

Lost and losing hope,
No Name

Age five began my earnest quest for a special dog companion. I turned on my blue eyed, blonde pig-tailed charm at all major holidays and birthdays, constantly begging and pleading for a four-legged canine friend. Christmas disappointments became all too frequent when a new basketball, Care Bear or craft kit replaced the yellow ball of cuddly fur I so fervently wished for under the tree.

I befriended every dog in the neighborhood. At the ripe age of seven I was already resident dog sitter and champion Milk Bone distributer to every dog in the Greater Boston area. Even though I worked tirelessly to develop a convincing argument, touting my only child status and the need for companionship, I was always told NO! Lame reasons (excuses) given included the hectic family schedule and a lack of extra quality time to properly devote to puppy. Able to finally twist mom and dad's arm just a tad during my sophomore-junior year of high school, we raised a black lab, named Ocoee, for Guiding Eyes for the Blind. Unfortunately he was mine, only on loan, and had to be tearfully returned after eighteen months of socialization and TLC.

I promised my young self that once I entered college, a big yellow Labrador would be my first adult purchase.

Murphy is now five. He is my best friend and dutiful shadow. Murph has taught me the greatest of life's lessons: the meaning of the word unconditional, how to always be a loyal friend and that absolute love is best expressed through a simple lick, cuddle and gaze into a set of big, brown, compassion-filled saucer eyes. He has also humbled my fashion pride, as I can never wear black without the accent of yellow and white pervasive dog hairs!

I'm now looking to expand my canine family so a new little pal can learn from Murphy, take on his mannerisms and endearing qualities, keep him spry and offer him friendship, company and love when I am not physically present. The thought of living a single day without loveable Murph

spirals me into panic. Knowing I could position a sweet, successor puppy in the wings, to grow up in the big guy's likeness, gives my heart a slight ember of solace and peace when I fearfully think about the inevitable ill-fated day when my best friend crosses the Rainbow Bridge.

Scrolling through thousands of thumbnail Internet images and bios of adoptable canine cuties, I found you. A little yellow dog from Viola, Tennessee simply named "Jake Yellow". Your kind eyes and signature racing stripe dancing perfectly down the middle of your face stole my expectant heart. I swiftly filled out all required paperwork and scheduled a home visit with Great Dog rescue, believing wholeheartedly that you were the missing piece to complete my family. After a lengthy interview with two dedicated rescue volunteers and a home visit evaluation for potential puppy hazards, I was given the go-ahead. You were cleared to leave your Southern home for a new life as a Bostonian.

The pre-adoption trip to Pet Smart was gleeful! I purchased a myriad of puppy essentials (and non-essentials) namely "woofies", poop bags, bones galore and of course a divine purple puppy collar and matching leash for your pick up in Plainfield, Connecticut. A total extravagant splurge! You, however, deserve the very best!

The most difficult part of the pre-adoption procedure proved to be the heart-to-heart talk I had with Murphy. When told of your impending arrival, he was very much concerned and conflicted, unable to fully comprehend why his five-year "only-child stint" was coming to an abrupt, unforeseen halt. Murph was a tough sell initially, but I assured him that before long the two of you would be kindred buddies. He too is blonde in color, enjoys walks, perfectly executes any trick for a "woofie" and has cemented himself as my permanent bed partner and best friend. As long as you don't jockey for excessive late night snuggle time right away, I assure you all will be copasetic. He will quickly welcome his new role as big brother and role model.

Fervently, I promise you a treasured, memorable life, abundantly rich with love, tenderness, adventures, fun and good care. April 30th is your adoption day. Chapter One of our story will now excitingly be written. Travel safe, little one. Can't wait to meet you. You better like purple and how about those Red Sox!?

Love,
Aislynn

To my new family,                                                April 23, 2005

Sorry for my bad handwriting and imperfect grammar. A young pup, I'm learning and will surely get better with practice and some real good teaching.

While sunning myself in the perfect dirt hole at Miss Emily's in good ole Viola, a gruff voice shouted "Jake Yellow, here boy". I'd been given that name when I was dropped here a few weeks ago. Always wanting to do what I was told, I hustled towards the large man who stood with a dangling leash in his right hand and set of keys in his left. I've watched dozens of pups leave with this strange man but never come back. Where was he gonna take me? Last time I went in the car was to visit the mobile neutering clinic. Believe me when I tell you that wasn't the best time. Ouch!

The shady character also took my brother, Yellow Sam. Only my third time in a car, the combination of dirt road bumpiness, cigar smoke and the constant

**THE SPAY STATION**
*"Saving Lives Through Prevention"*
The Humane Association of Wilson County, POB 2130, Lebanon, TN 37088 (615)444-1196

**SPAY/NEUTER & VACCINATION RECORD**

Date  2.24.05

Jake ____ Dillman ____ your ☒DOGS ☐CAT was ☐SPAYED ☒NEUTERED
(pet's name)          (owner's last name)

And also received the following vaccinations:

☒ 1 Year Rabies Vaccine (certificate attached)

☐ Eclipse *3 (Feline Rhinotracheitis-Calici-Panleukopenia Vaccine, Modified Live Virus)
*Your cat received an injection of ivermectin for parasites. You may see round worms (they look like spaghetti) come out in stool.

☒ Galaxy*DA2PPv (Canine Distemper-Adenovirus Type 2-Parainfluenza-Parvovirus Vaccine, Modified Live Virus)

Other _____

It is the client's responsibility to keep this record on file. The Spay Station does not revaccinate.
**FOR SPAY/NEUTER RELATED EMERGENCIES ONLY** CALL (615)708-1233, 444-9979 OR 330-6372

splashing sound of a large coffee swirling around a stained Styrofoam cup was unsettling to churn my anxious stomach. Plus, I had no idea where we were heading, though I sought some comfort knowing my brother was with me! Can't stop thinking bout Ma and my other siblings though. Hope they get a real chance, especially Ma, though I reckon it's hard getting folks to take in older, more elderly mutts.

Sam and me desperately tried to listen to the men up front talking, but it was hard to hear amongst the blaring Country Western tunes. Heard somethin' about an 18-wheeler heading up to New England. We arrived in Knoxville after a few hours and the two guys gathered some paperwork, gave us a rough yet endearing rub on the noggin and said, "Be good and enjoy the family life. Ya'll the lucky ones."

I've spent my entire puppyhood trying to survive. Been educated hard knocks style. I ain't got skills, no formal training, look pretty ragged and ain't sure I deserve family life. I'm over the moon grateful for a chance, and sure as dickens promise to give ya'll my best, learn how to be good in a home and become your loyal companion.

Farewell Viola. Just hope Ma and my friends at Miss Emily's also catch a break for a new beginning.

> From,
> Yellow Jake

---

**CERTIFICATE OF RABIES VACCINATION**
**TENNESSEE DEPARTMENT OF HEALTH**

State Tag No. 576029      County Registration No. _____

This is to certify that the   Dog ☒   Cat ☐   Date 2.24.05   owned by:

Emily Dillman   County Warren

Address 300 Allendale Blvd, McMinnville, TN 37110

on the above date was vaccinated against rabies.   Phone 931-668-0770

Breed Lab Mix   Name Jake

Color yellow   Sex N/Male   Weight 25#   Dosage 1cc

Live Virus ☐

Vaccine Manufacturer Schering   Type: Killed Virus ☒

Lot No. M473763   Date for Revaccination 2.24 06

_Julia Adams_   D.V.M.

This certificate shall be kept by the person who owns, keeps or harbors the said dog or cat at all times subject to the inspection of the proper county officer.

Form PH-1650 (R 1/98)   White - Pet Owner   Yellow - Health Department   Blue - Veterinarian   RDA 629

Dear Yellow Jake,

The long anticipated day has finally arrived!! Your grandma, also so eager to meet you, enthusiastically joined me on the 2-hour drive to Plainfield to make your acquaintance. We packed the red Land Rover with all the comforts of home: blankets, treats, a few plush toys, a Kodak disposal camera, your new purple leash set and even a few plain Dunkin' Donuts munchkins, Murph's favorite, as a special welcoming treat just for you.

We located the Park-n-Ride area and saw other families loitering, leashes and collars in hand, anxiously waiting to also meet their new four-legged best friends for the first time. A hush came over the parking area as we watched the big 18-wheeler truck make a wide turn and park in the open space. A thin man wearing dirty overalls and a red and white ripped flannel button down stumbled out of the truck and started calling dog names.

"Jake's people!!" he shouted. I eagerly and boldly moved myself to the front of the line. Your grandma was positioned right behind to snap the perfect photo of our initial meeting. The driver awkwardly held you up Lion King style, and with trepidation in your eyes you surveyed the crowd of people standing before you. You got dropped, rather maladroitly in my waiting arms and despite being yellowish in color, you looked nothing like the tiny photograph I fell in love with online. You were covered with mange, had tar caked in your ears and bucked frantically when I tried to put your purple collar around your neck. The driver said "Ma'am – this dog ain't never been on no leash before" and in that moment with you uncontrollably foraging the parking lot for hardened french fries from the nearby McDonalds, crumpled tissues, and other assorted, unknown highway rubbish delectables I thought: what have I gotten myself into? I suddenly remembered my high school Latin: Caveat Emptor!

Confused and Worried,
Aislynn & Grandma

Dear new family,                                                    April 30, 2005

The ride from Viola to Plainfield was bumpy, dark and long. Rickety crates were stacked six high and filled the whole big rig. Truck was carrying almost 500 pups. The sound of clashing metal was frightening and kept lots of us scared. Howling, barking and whimpering created a sad yet soulful evening soundtrack, one that after day four on the road lulled me to a fitful sleep. Thought about Ma a lot and prayed to God she and my siblings were called on the next truckload departure.

We made lots of stops along the way but weren't given a chance to tinkle. All us tried to hold it, but everyone had an unfortunate accident or two along the way. Driver'd yell and angrily shake the crate if we relieved ourselves. Grumbling under his breath he'd take a spray bottle full of chemicals, aim it through the metal bars, and disinfect the soil. He ain't never took the time to get us out of the crate, instead we were made to sit amongst toxic cleaning mist, urine and feces. When we hit bumps or made wide turns, liquid waste would seep out the sides of the crates and pool on the floor below. All our dignity was lost.

Them set up a fan with batteries to move some rancid air round but it idled on its side most of the time having been jostled about by speed bumps and herky jerky driving. Smell of messes, mangy furred pups and tobacco smoke created a rank odor that'll stay with me forever.

At each stop, the driver'd slowly pace the narrow walking space of our quarters, always fumbling through a pile of tattered papers making pencil notations between the lines. He'd eye us one by one. Then, after scribbling the correct identification hastily open the correct metal crates, loop at makeshift lasso-like leash around our neck and carry us to the cockpit of the truck where he began calling out names at random. I relied on my keen, almond-shaped eyes to watch the behavior of the driver, but the stark, linear cage bars obstructed my view and made it hard to make sense of his shuffle. I do know that the pups that left with this elderly character never got brought back. Wonderment and anxiety escalated. Where were they headed? We next? They getting families like the cigar smoking guys told us about in Tennessee?

After nearly six days on the road, the odd driver stumbled along the aisle, and ID'd me and Sam, a task becoming easier and easier by the mile as more pups been leaving the rig. They say us dogs got no sense of time, but believe me when I tell you we know a long, long while. Needing to pee real bad and feeling pretty woozy, he clumsily held Sam and me under his armpit and walked us to the makeshift stairs resting upside the passenger side door. With glassy, unfocused, tired eyes I surveyed the crowd of humans lurking before me. Though not of clear head, they seemed to be gawking and passing non-verbal judgment of my cockeyed ears, imperfect coat, and thin frame.

The man released his hold and I was clumsily dropped in your arms. You smelled flower fresh and I was worried my fouled fur would sully your clean, white top. Broadly smiling, your giddy excitement traveled through my anxious, limp bones like an unwavering, dynamic electric current and filled me with a curious sense of calm and safety. You stood tall, proud and claimed me as your own even though I didn't look my best. Grandma hovered behind snapping countless photos with a blinding flash. You fastened a collar around my neck and articulated all sorts of commands like "Easy", "Heel", "Wait". I had no idea what you were talking about. I think Miss Emily might have stretched the truth to folks about our learning skills to try to get people to consider us Tennessee dogs.

Exhausted from the never-ending, terrifying ride, I sought comfort being in a cozy, smaller vehicle even though I was still confused and unsure of my final destination. You made a constant fuss over me, rubbing my ears and offering me bacon-flavored yummies that I ain't never before tasted. After a short while of fighting off sleep, I circled the backseat and plopped down, relaxin' up against your khaki shorts. I rested my elongated snout on your lap and closed my weary eyes. I became hypnotized by your constant, gentle, comforting touch along my white racing stripe; a nice departure from the wailing I'd become accustomed to falling asleep to during my journey. I awoke in front of a big grey house. Norfolk, Massachusetts was the endpoint. You kissed my snout and said, "Welcome home, little one." Home. I was home. A real home at last!

You picked me! Out of thousands of little pictures on a computer screen. You literally saved my life. Gave me hope. I'm so grateful, though I ain't got the right words to say it. I can offer you nothin' but my best and will show my appreciation for your kindness and love everyday. I'll love unconditionally. Cheer you up when you're down. Wag my tail when you need a smile. Lick your face to express joy and be your steady friend til the final beat of my heart. That is my sincere promise.

With appreciation,
Yellow Jake

---

Jake

### Great Dog Rescue New England
### Health Requirement Checklist

*FAX TO 901-767-6728 no later than Sunday!*

| | ITEM | DATE | VETERINARIAN NAME AND TELEPHONE |
|---|---|---|---|
| δ | Health Certificate dated within 10 days of transport. | 4/25 | Name Mcminnville Animal Care TEL (931) 473-2533 |
| δ | Spay/neuter certificate | 2/24 | Name The Spay Station TEL (615) 444-1196 |
| δ | Rabies vaccine and rabies certificate | 2/24 | Name The Spay Station TEL (615) 444-1196 |
| δ | Bordatello vaccine at least 10 days prior to transport. | 4/2 | Name Foster TEL (931) 635-2765 |
| δ | DHLPP for adult dogs | 2/24 | Name The Spay Station TEL (615) 444-1196 |
| δ | FIRST 5-in-1 puppy shot | | Name TEL ( ) |
| δ | SECOND 5-in-1 puppy shot at least 10 days prior to transport | 2/10 | Name Foster TEL (931) 635-2765 |
| δ | THIRD 5-in-1 puppy shot (optional if no time before transport) | | Name TEL ( ) |
| δ | FIRST puppy deworming with Strongid | 2/10 | Name Foster TEL (931) 635-2765 |
| δ | SECOND puppy deworming with Strongid | 2/11 | Name Foster TEL (931) 635-2765 |
| δ | THIRD puppy deworming with Strongid | 2/12 | Name Foster TEL (931) 635-2765 |
| δ | Adult dog deworming with Drontal Panacur 4/21 & 4/22 | 4/2 | Name Foster TEL (931) 635-2765 |
| δ | HW / lyme / ehrlichia test Negative | 4/23 | Name Mcminnville Animal Care TEL (931) 473-2533 |

Affix labels from med bottle if puppy shots given by foster mom.

2/10/05

4/2/05

---

12

Dear Yellow Jake,                                                                April 30, 2005

Welcome home!

Prior to picking you up, I Googled the best way to have you meet your big brother Murphy to alleviate potential turf and dominance issues at the house. I was advised to have the first meet and greet in a neutral schoolyard, that's why you met your new brother at H.O Day School, not at home. Wanted to explain that to you because I am sure you thought it rather strange. Though

you were both rather unsure and aloof, I was pleased with the initial meeting and sincerely believe you'll soon be fast friends. Murph will come around and quickly welcome you into the fold. You two will create a golden brotherhood!

You learned the rules and expectations of home life very swiftly and appear very fond of the daily routine. You quickly learned where the "woofie" jar was, took to looking out the first floor windows to assess the comings and goings of suburban neighborhood life, were trained on the Invisible Fence in a matter of days offering outdoor freedoms and enjoyed resting the afternoons away atop a pillow soft chair, with a direct beam of sunlight coming in through the window to warm your blonde fur.

I know how embarrassed you felt after accidentally tinkling on the new sateen Restoration Hardware curtains. Housebreaking has been our biggest challenge to date, but it's not your fault. For six months you were never in one place long enough to learn proper bathroom etiquette and just went where and when you felt moved. We'll get there. Don't feel bad. Curtains are replaceable; you are not.

Changing the name Yellow Jake to something more personal was the next task. I came up with a handful of names that seemed fitting given your personality, but thought it only appropriate for you to choose your own name. I'll never forget our time at the playground. "Chance! Here boy! Chancey!!!", "Brewster, Brewster, Come!". This went on for what seemed like hours until I yelled: "Sully!!!" With an immediate bounce in your step, you sprinted my way and in that fateful moment, you became Sullivan, never again to be referred to as Yellow Jake. That said, as a reminder of your humble Southern beginnings, your initial Tennessee Jake tag hangs from your purple collar amongst your new, shiny Norfolk bling.

It's starting to come together,
Aislynn

Dear Mom,                                                          September 1, 2005

I totally dig car rides and love running free!

Car rides are awesome! Even if just a co-pilot for company, I love riding with my head fully out the window, the wind expanding my jowls. I always keep my eyes out for cement trucks and motorcycles, and give a confident bark of gratitude, remembering those kind souls who gave me some food and hope when I was trying to survive on the Interstate 40.

I play a little game after returning home from fun car rides. After being let out of the car, I stand at full attention in the driveway; staring at the garage door. I wait, still and stoic, for you to press the magical button that opens the garage door. Once the door begins to rise, I leap the stonewall and lap the house in full sprint to see if I'm fast enough to "beat the garage door", returning to my starting point before the door has fully risen. Though the garage door has managed a few wins over time, I'm proud to say I typically come out victorious.

My roots with Miss Emily run deep. I enjoy spending relaxing afternoons lying on the blacktop driveway or lounging in the back end of the car, trunk door fully raised for visibility and breeze. I snooze the afternoons away, or attentively patrol the comings and goings of the neighborhood. I also keep my eyes peeled for the unsuspecting squirrel. After all, that type of challenging chase really does me good!

Jaunts to the reservoir are my favorite. That three-mile round trip, off-leash walk in Weston does my exercise regimen and heart good. Believe me when I tell you I indeed heard every one of your fright filled "Sully!!!" alarm shouts when you thought I'd run off, but I was always within earshot. I've improved on command recall and have learned to stay close, thanks to Murph's steady example. Remaining focused was the unspoken obedience expectation, but doing so on a wooded path of sheer wonder and adventure; with sights, sounds and smells abounding, was far too much for this little guy to handle. Darting in and out of the trail path, making the acquaintance of new and diverse

furry friends, splashing in the natural streams, sprinting after chipmunks and barking at geese offered the recipe for a perfect, carefree day. Every time we go, I fall just a little bit more in love with my unbridled freedom, and ability to run fast and uninhibited.

You should call me "wheels",
Sully

I am so happy and proud to spend our first Christmas together. A white Christmas, I will never forget the look of joy on your face and uncontrolled excitement when you ran through the snow for the first time! It came all the way up to your belly and you leapt like a jackrabbit to

hurdle yourself from one snowdrift to the other. Sheer joy! Wanting to bring you in the house to dry the frozen flakes from your fur, you stoically stood in the tallest mound, tongue at full extension flopping from your mouth, looking so proud and happy. I ran to warm up by the fire, and pour a small glass of Egg Nog, allowing you to savor just a few more moments in the wintery wonderland.

It took you a few days to feel okay about the Christmas tree. At first I think you thought it an indoor tinkle repository, but once the lights and other adornments graced the boughs you were able to separate decoration from urinary function.

You seemed most enthused by your stocking stuffers and wrapped gifts. Chewy treats and soft bones perfect for your sensitive, small teeth overflowed from the brim of your hand-knit stocking. A plethora of Cape Cod inspired preppy collars/leash combos embellished with whales, bees and watermelons were perfectly wrapped in boxes of all size. Your grandma kindly created a book of memories for you, chock full of photos, adoption papers and the like, documenting our near first year together. What a special collection of memories to reflect upon from time to time.

You looked at me with sheer perplexity as you opened your final gift; a DNA kit. You were a champ while I swabbed your cheek. I know it was uncomfortable, but I know you enjoyed your post swipe potato skin chaser. Not knowing your breed ancestry, I trust this test will offer some clarity as to your mix and help me exercise proactivity and prudence regarding potential future medical concerns or treatment choices. Though you're my adored Heinz 57 lab-mix, the results reflect traces of Standard Poodle, Corgi and Dachshund. These breeds seem rather farfetched and even eclectic, but resemblance is apparent upon close observation. At the end of the day you are my beloved, Sully. Nothing more, nothing less. Truly one of a kind!

A huge thank you, my sweet boy, for your most outstanding and thoughtful handmade gift. Placed in prominence on the family room bookshelf, your framed paw print and photomontage will always make me smile and feel eternally grateful our paths crossed. I will forever treasure it.

Thanks for making this the best Christmas ever,

Aislynn

P.S. Our neighbors Beth and Chris think you resemble Santa's Little Helper from the Simpsons. What do you think?

It's been a year since my eventful adoption! My learning curve has been high, and I've worked hard to fine-tune my penmanship, vocabulary and writing.

I will always be a Southerner at heart even though my accent and drawl is waning. I'm confident I'll never adopt the silly talk of the folks here in "the Bean". Cah, wicked and Fluffa Nutta! Silly talk!

Life in Norfolk is nothing like rural Tennessee, that's for sure. I've come to thankfully expect two heaping helpings of food each day, unlimited water, "woofies", bones and even ice cream on special days! I really hope Sam is being treated just as well. You initially expected me to sleep in a crate but it was just too reminiscent of the traumatic truck ride up from the south. The bitter metal smell and reverberating clatter heard as I circled to find a comfortable spot was just too much to remember and bear. I've since developed an overpowering fondness for the oversized, comfy chair in the family room. I love burrowing under my violet blanket, finding the perfect spot suitable for an afternoon cat nap or evening slumber. Don't think I could ask for anything more. Only wish Ma and all the pups at Miss Emily's could be treated like this. A simple life. A good life. A cherished life.

Thanks for enrolling me in obedience class. It's amazing how quickly I was able to pick up the basic commands. I really enjoy walking on the leash with you but love running free at the reservoir with Murph. Though I was bothered by the intrusiveness of my veterinary exam, I am grateful

that a little medication and change in food has made my fur look good, cleared up my ears, and added some meat to my bones. I know I'll never have Murph's pedigree purebred, polished look, but hope you'll love me just the same.

I love baked potatoes. Howl when the answering machine picks up missed calls. "Sing" the soprano line to Big Murph's baritone whenever you play Beethoven's "Moonlight Sonata" on the piano. Adore spending time with my grandma who spoils me rotten and unconditionally accepts my sometimes aloof ways. Live for jaunts to Bubbling Brook for a kiddy cup of homemade vanilla ice cream. Most importantly, I can't seem to wipe the I LOVE LIFE smile off my face whenever I am with you. Thank you! Thank you!

I love my new name. Sullivan. It represents a fresh start, a new beginning. What really makes me grin inside is when you call me other special, adorable, personalized nicknames. That's when I know I'm really loved. I'd always hear you call Murphy silly, endearing names like Murphlet and Em and thought, when

is she gonna say something notable like that to me? The first time you called me "Sylvie" and "Straussie" I knew I was yours. My heart did a dance!

I love Norfolk,
Straussie

Dear little brother, May 13, 2009

Truth be told, I wasn't so excited when I first learned you were headed to Norfolk. You know what they say: two's company, three's a crowd.

But was I wrong.
You have been such a great add. Love that we have each other to hang out with when Ais is seeing clients or on the road. True we spend much of the day catching zzzzz's, but I enjoy the quiet time we spend bonding, sharing secrets and watching trashy daytime television. You know how I feel about "The View". Gonna have to talk to Ais about not leaving the television on Channel 5 all day. Those women are crazy!

You've even been able to win over Papa Scott, no easy task there, as a slow(er) lover of dogs! I know you're grandma's favorite and think it's cute how she takes you on special rides, walks and even brings you to school to show you off to her kiddos!

My life got better when you came. That's the truth!

We are writing the book on Golden Family Values,
Big Murph

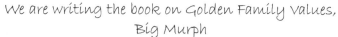

21

Dear Mom,

Please have children soon because I am tired of having to dress up as a pumpkin with Murph every Halloween.
BOO,
Sully

Dear Sully,                                                            November 21, 2010

I am so proud of you.

You are such a blessing to the guests at the Abundant Table. While these needy individuals and families attend for a free hot meal, they truly hunger for judgment-free love and acceptance. Gentle and loving, you provide that and then some. You graciously allow the guests to hug and walk you. Often unaware of what's always right, they unknowingly pull your tail or inadvertently poke your eyes. You never respond in frustration or anger and are always gracious and most patient.

Though you adore the special attention and land a few extra table scraps out of the deal,

your heart is big and you need to know that your ability to brighten the days of the sick, disadvantaged downtrodden and soften the souls of the hardhearted is truly remarkable. You are making a real difference in their lives.

Thanks for being you,
Aislynn

Dear Mom,                                                                April 5, 2011

Now I know how Murphy must have felt on April 30, 2005 when I suddenly came on the scene. Murph and I make quite the dynamic duo, the

golden brotherhood is solid. I'm really not sure why you felt the need to add this new, small, yellow, impish character into the mix. You've named him Brown, though he should've been called "Dickens". That ruffian is trouble. He's the type of hooligan that steals kids lunch money!

Okay, I enjoy chasing him around the front yard holly bush and think its amusing how he tries to keep up with me at the reservoir; but watching him eat rocks and kitchen counter surf for plastic bags and sweet treats – now that's where I draw the line. The kid's a newbie and he's been to Tufts Emergency Hospital already twice in his young life. I'll talk to the rascal, but can't promise miracles. He's an accident waiting to happen.

My saving grace is that Brown likes his "studio" crate residence as it gives Big Murph and me the opportunity to veg, uninterrupted, take in some extra private Ais snuggle time, enjoy head massages and catch up on DVR'd Bravo sleaze.

Frustrated but keeping an open
mind about this rookie,
Sully

Dear Mom,                                          June 5, 2011

I had the best time kayaking with you today. I was a little concerned the

life vest would make me look weird, but I am glad I wore it. Just in case, you know. After all, I barely earned my entry-level Guppy Swimming certificate!

Loved lying at your feet scanning the freshwater landscape: turtles sunning themselves on floating logs, young signets swiftly following their mother's lead and watching an imposing heron land from flight. So cool too that I could bend down and take a quick drink from the Charles River whenever I felt parched. Nature's water bowl!

I think it's awesome that this is something that we can do together, just us. I can't wait until we go out again. Though next time how about you leave the audio speakers in the car. You know I

also enjoy a good country playlist, but I'm not sure how prepped the wildlife of the Charles were to hear your pipes singing along. Let's just enjoy nature's symphony, huh? Love spending treasured alone time with you. Makes me feel so special. When can we go again? How about Friday?

Keep paddling,
Sull

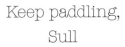

Dear Straussie,                                                      August 20, 2011

     I find myself writing with lessened regularity. The days and weeks seem to run together. I just don't know where the time goes. You continue to be the "steady eddy" of the family. Unwavering and loyal, you've beautifully cemented yourself as best friend, listener, confidante, middle brother, neighborhood sentinel, squirrel chaser and beloved grand dog.

     Underneath your independent exterior I see a soft, insecure, vulnerable soul always questioning adequacy and worth. I want you to know, dear boy that you have brought me nothing but joy and happiness since your Plainfield pick up. You are low maintenance, easy going and never demanding. You graciously show wholehearted appreciation for your adoption on a daily basis.

     You constantly compare yourself to Murph and Brownie and secretly wish for their straight teeth, pedigree lineage, upper-middle class Franklin, Massachusetts roots and revered American Kennel Club registration. Listen when I tell you, little one, that you are the creamy, white middle stability to an Oreo cookie of emotionally needy purebred labs. Murph is deeply sensitive, Brown a magnet for trouble. You are a rock, steadfast and true.

     Your three, uniquely wonderful personalities make you cherished, special, and extraordinarily lovable. My love for the brotherhood is equal, knows no limit and could never be hierarchically ranked.

     Your battle for survival was and is inspiring. You are a courageous fighter in perseverance and fortitude. Never lose your grit, for that is what I admire most about you.

I am truly looking forward to some uninterrupted, relaxing vacation time with my golden brotherhood. I know how much you love the new Jeep Wrangler. What do you say we take the doors off and go for a wind in our hair summer spin to Narragansett for a Brickley's ice cream cone?!

Always be my fighter,
Ais

Dear Mom,                                                        April 30, 2012

Today is my seven-year adoption anniversary! Can't believe it! I know much of who I am is because of my early life of struggle and hardship in Viola, but I am so happy now living with you and my bros! Life is good. I have been truly blessed. Couldn't ask for more. Just wish Ma could have come to Norfolk too.

The best is yet to be,
Sully

Dear Mom,                                          July 31, 2012

    I need you to call the vet. Please. Hurry!!

    I was running with Murph and Brown and all of a sudden my front left leg came up lame. You know I'm a pretty tough and resilient guy. I tried to shake it off, but I can't. Limping is the only way I can get around, and the pain – the excruciating pain is something terrible. Thought maybe I accidentally stepped on a cluster of stinging bees, or pulled a muscle out of place while chasing Brownie around the trampoline but I don't think so. This is a different type of pain. I really think something is wrong. Very wrong.

    I'm scared. Think Grandma might be able to come to the vet with us for some moral support?

Hurting and a little worried,

Sylvie

Dear Sullivan,                                                                              August 7, 2012

You have been such a brave trooper, my little friend. The last few weeks we have frequented the vet like Bostonians haunt Dunkin' Donuts, yet sadly, we still do not have a definitive clinical diagnosis or course of treatment for your ever-worsening leg ailment.

Lyme disease and other such tick-borne illnesses were ruled out through an intensive blood draw. Massage and chiropractic treatments at Sterling Impressions proved futile (though I know you enjoyed all the loving hands rubbing you in all your favorite spots), and the high prescribed doses of Tramadol and Gabapentin appeared to initially minimize your discomfort though over time proved just to be a pain mask.

Your walking is becoming evermore lame and labored. Squirrels no longer fear entrance into our yard. Malaise and lethargy have replaced your once quintessential playful and robust vein. We haven't been able to run the reservoir for weeks, and I cancelled the trip to your beloved Cape Cod fearing the travel might be too difficult for your ever-worsening ambulation.

Our most recent vet appointment was frightening and left me anxious and confused. After completing a relatively simple neurological examination, which forced you to endure terribly awkward manipulations of your neck and spine, the doctor proclaimed, "bet this dog has something neurological going on...but don't worry, I'm not talking cancer." Relieved to hear "no" to the dreaded "C word", other possible frightening diagnoses still threaten. I feel terrible having to put you through more pokes, prods and taps to unearth their lode, but alas, we need to get to the bottom of the problem.

Next week we go back for a specialized neck x-ray. With any luck, that will be conclusive in nature and the missing puzzle piece in defining this clinical jigsaw mystery. In the meantime, I will continue Googling everything and anything, hoping to stumble on something definitive that will quickly offer you restored health, pain relief and mobility freedom.

Though your tawny eyes reflect growing concern and weariness, I ask that you fight the fight. Be strong! I feel helpless, my friend. I so desperately want to do right by you and quickly take away your pain. We will get through this together. I promise. I'll be with you every step of the way. You are an integral part of a solid golden brotherhood and hold the love, admiration and best wishes of many.

Keep fighting,
Aislynn

Dear Mom,                                                        August 13, 2012

Ugh! Definitely still woozy. I'm just beginning to come to after a very confusing and eventful afternoon. Memory fuzz plus the lingering sedation meds are making the day hard to process, but believe me when I tell you today was awful!

I remember being anxious to go to the vet. Butterflies danced in my belly the whole foreboding ride to Walpole, and once we arrived, nerves elevated even more. We lingered in the waiting room for a few minutes, the sound of the secretary typing and fidgeting with a candy wrapper the only audible din. After popping a root beer smelling something in her mouth and moving it to rest on the side of her cheek she said, "Go to Room 1".

We waited in the small, dingy room until a woman dressed in baggy scrubs came in holding a plastic case of fluid with an uber long needle attached to the tip. Without even giving me a reassuring introductory hello pat, or even taking a second to check my chart to learn my real name rather than calling me "boy"; she tented my neck scruff, inserted the ginormous needle and said, "Good boy" in a very indifferent drone. You were comfortingly rubbing my white shoulder blades and humming a somewhat recognizable Wynonna tune while the surge of cold fluid radiated through my tense body.

My eyes grew heavy; my pink tongue hung limply out of my mouth and I felt myself getting groggy. Upon falling asleep, the needle-holding person came back in and asked that we move to a different examination room. She grabbed my leash and attempted to drag my deadweight, somewhat lifeless self into another room until you angrily stopped her. You tenderly bent down, positioned your long arms under my midsection and carried my heavy body down the hall – muttering under your breath. Your hair falling in your face, I felt occasional puffs of air tickle my fur as you tried to blow the loose strands from your eyes to see which room we were expected to enter. Though quite loopy, I'm not sure why we had to switch rooms. The waiting room was empty, the technicians were on lunch break and the only other patient in the hospital was a squawking bird, who appeared equally unhappy with the lack of compassionate care, given its ongoing verbal, nonsensical protests. Insensitivity. Gruff and Harsh.

Ma always told us that 'only kindness matters'. This veterinary establishment could use a lesson in kindness, sensitivity and gentility from my Ma. Though a mangy stray, without formal training or pedigree, her whole life was dedicated to caring for and protecting others. Ma lived compassion and barked love.

After the x-ray I was still very much stoned, and laid at your feet while you spoke to the vet and disinterested receptionist. Despite being confused and bewildered, I could tell by your increased foot shuffling, blunt dialogue and iPhone fumbling that your frustration, emotionality and impatience was elevating. You were holding back tears. You said, "Come on Sylvie…Let's go." I tried to muster the energy to move, but was unsteady. The vet and secretary idly and unsympathetically watched as you fumbled to carry me to the car, your struggle to open the door very apparent.

My fur caught your tears. You gently placed me on a purple polka-dotted blanket in the back seat and gave me a comforting ear rub and kiss on the nose. We sat in the parking lot for a few minutes. I snoozed, but knew you turned on the radio to drown out your sobbing. I am sorry you had to attend this important appointment alone. You need a big hug. I just wish I had been awake enough to hear what the vet told you. Couldn't have been good.

Still dazed and confused,
Sullivan

My sweet, brave Sullivan,                                                    August 13, 2012

Today was one of the hardest days of my life. I am so sorry, my friend, that you were faced with such indifference and apathy. This inexcusable absence of kindness, ongoing lack of medical due-diligence professionalism and inability to refer out for a second opinion when uncertainty trumped knowledge is why we will never return to Walpole for veterinary care.

Your x-ray was inconclusive. A "slight abnormality of disc space" the report.

While laying on the cold floor, sedated, the vet said, "It's very clear to me that Sullivan is in a good amount of pain. You, his loving owner and companion, need to now decide how long you want him to live this way." Staring blankly in her direction, mind reeling I thought: What is she saying? Tests are inconclusive. No diagnosis. No answers. But I'm being prepped for your passing? What is the basis for this opinion?

Before I could cogently form a follow up reply, she began telling me of her dog Sadie's battle with pain. Sadie lives for going out for walks and shows uncontrolled excitement when the leash surfaces from behind the closet door. Though the walks are slow, and Sadie comes home stiff and tired, the time out is worth every tinge of discomfort and fatigue. The vet went on to say that should the day come when Sadie does not get excited to go for a walk, the sight of sneakers getting laced and the front door opening wide does not tickle her fancy, only then would she know it's Sadie's appointed time.

After wrapping up her story, the doctor handed me a card for Dr. Alicia Karas, the top specialist in pain management from Tufts Veterinary hospital and said, "call her. It's what's best for Sully."

I was perfunctorily asked to pay the bill by the cheeky aide with wire-rimmed glasses and after scribbling my name on the receipt, stuck the folded wad of paperwork and Dr. Karas's card between my clenched teeth. I then reached down to carry you to the car as you were still too medicated to steadily and independently walk outside. The doctor and staff unsympathetically watched as I struggled to open the door. Tears blurred my vision. My long bangs fell in my face. Your deadweight body was cumbersome. No one offered to help. No one cared. No words of encouragement given.

I cried in the car, replaying the doctor's callous counsel over and over again in my mind: Keep Sully comfortable until it's his time.

After a cathartic, tearful release I ripped Dr. Karas's card in small and smaller pieces, wiped my tears and started making mental action plan notes as to who could open appropriate medical doors and offer required GPS navigation down a diagnostic path to get you the best and most compassionate treatment.

   We are family little man. We stick together. No one left behind. We will figure out what's ailing your leg and stop at nothing to ensure many more reservoir runs and playful chases with Brown around the holly bush.

We are a team,
Ais

Dear Sully,                                          August 14, 2012

This morning I received a kind text from our friend and neighbor, Katie Adams, inquiring about your left leg and overall wellbeing. I shared with her briefly about our disappointing vet visit and she said, "You've gotta go to Angell Medical Center."

Not sure if you remember, but her little yellow mutt, Harry, was treated at Angell after his small dust up with a bigger, aggressive canine a few months back. Harry broke his fibula and required surgery. Dr. Brum brilliantly executed Harry's procedure and outfitted him in a little green cast that you and your brothers signed. Katie can't say enough about her Angell experience and specifically raves about the hyper-professionalism and compassionate care with which they consistently perform.

Katie generously offered to make a few preliminary phone calls to see if Dr. Brum ASAP could see us. We have every reason to confidently believe that the talented people at Angell will be able to diagnose your problem and offer an effective holistic treatment plan.

Angell is a world renowned comprehensive, all-inclusive animal hospital. Emergency doctors, surgeons, neurologists, radiologists, oncologists, pain specialists and the like are on staff at all times ready to collegially collaborate with each other to determine best practices care.

Just called. It's a miracle. We have an appointment scheduled for tomorrow. I truly believe this is a major breakthrough step in the right direction. I know in my heart they will direct our path to the most favorable treatment plan possible.

Anxious but holding on to hope,

Aislynn

Dear Katie,                                                                                    August 14, 2012

You are a miracle worker. We just received a call from Angell. Sully has an appointment with Dr. Johns and Dr. Brum tomorrow morning.

Praying that we will finally gain some medical clarity.

Thank you a million times. Please give my four-legged god pup, Harry, a big kiss on the head and let him know that his godmother loves him very much.

I dream of the day sweet Sully can run again. Fast. Free. Without pain. A permanent smile plastered on his yellow face. His brothers and Harry panting yards behind, unable to keep up.

That will be a joyous day. A festive party. Frosty Paw treats on me!

Six months. He'll be able to run freely in six months. Wanna make that bet?

You've opened the biggest door,<br>
Ais

Dear Mom,                                                          August 15, 2012

I don't want to wallow, but today I'm feeling sad and discouraged. Woke up this morning and took a momentary glance down, and felt dread seeing the ominous, incredible atrophy in my front left leg. I cannot believe the considerable, rapid loss of muscle mass and sheer deterioration of strength. My front leg muscles used to be bulging. I'd draw envious stares and whispering romantic compliments from impressionable young female pups all the time! Now, skin and bones. How did this happen? No more lustful looks!

Today may be the day hard questions will be answered and a treatment plan developed, but right now I feel devastated. I can't run. I can barely walk, not without a considerable limp and knuckling. I've been ingesting pills like Murph devours "woofies". I've been forced to be a spectator in life rather than an active participant. Promise they will come up with a treatment plan? I just don't know how much longer I can live like this. Uncertainty. Unknowns.

Woah! Angell is a beautiful place! Loved how the automatic doors opened upon my approach – way cool! The greeter was super nice, gave me a real heartfelt pat and sent me over to the dog waiting area where I met two other pups waiting for appointments. Cats climbing on a carpeted play place in the adoption center caught my eye, as did the hazy, hot and humid five-day weather forecast projected by the Channel 5 meteorologist on television. The hospital is so very clean. Men and women with mops continuously pass by like clockwork splashing lavender smelling fragrance over the floors, while others Windex nose prints off the windows and glass doors.

Pups from all walks of life are coming in and out of this place. A brindle greyhound, wearing a hot pink cast on her back leg on having endured a

38

chemotherapy treatment, lurked in the waiting area waiting for her "person" to book another appointment, a small, newly adopted Boston Terrier named Valentine was waiting for his battery of puppy shots; and a silly, guilty looking chocolate lab named Tisbury sat to my right for an Ultrasound after ingesting dill pickles and Godiva chocolate. Hey, Brown, you might have met your match! A watcher of pups and people, my wait in the waiting room was amusing and calmed my flip-flopping stomach. Your hands never stopped stroking my body, and every so often you'd pluck out a tuft or two of loose, shedding fur and let it fall to the floor. I'm told dogs molt when nervous. Miracle I'm not yet bald!

"Sullivan?" a woman's voice queried? I stumbled a little to get up, and stood before the white-coated woman who gave me a friendly greeting. Kind, she made a big deal of my signature racing stripe, and thought it funny how my tail wagged in circles!

Once we got into the exam room, the doctor, who identified herself as Dr. Johns, asked you and grandma a whole lot of questions. She got down on the ground, gave me TLC and whispered a few sweet nothings in my ear. I think she likes me! Her exam was so thorough and lasted nearly an hour. Checked everything. After each manipulation and observation, she stood up and typed her findings into a small computer, about the size of a Milk Bone box. Her pockets were full of shiny medical, cold instruments and woofies. Murph would have had his nose in her coat! She offered me a few peanut butter smelling bones, but I turned my nose to these delectables given my nervous belly.

Harry's friend Dr. Brum came in for a quick cameo, gave me a once over and the two discussed my case. Tired, I rested on the chilly floor, head propped on your calf, while the doctors chatted with you and grandma. My ears suddenly stood at attention when possible diagnoses were shared: cancer, immune-mediated illness, polyarthritis or orthopedic problems. Cancer? Didn't the Walpole vet rule out cancer? I don't understand. Could I really have cancer? Think Sam has these types of problems too? No wonder people don't want to risk taking in mix-breed Southern pups from Tennessee.

The next step was explained, though I was mentally in and out, totally distracted by what I just heard. I stared blankly at a wall full of medical instruments and a laminated paper reading: Today's Pollen Count.

I was to be swept off for more testing. Dr. Johns took off my maroon collar with embroidered bees, and handed it to you for safekeeping. She then slipped a loose fitting blue leash around my neck, reminiscent of what the Tennessee transport truck driver used after prying us out of our crates. Grandma offered a quiet, fervent prayer and you gave me a tight hug, though neither gesture calmed my quaking insides. Trying to be brave, I left with the white-coated doctor and was led down a large, dimly lit hall without a clue of what was to happen, how long I'd be, and what information would be sought.

They made me pee in a cup and poked me for blood samples. My chest, lumbar spine, c-spine and thorax were x-rayed. I had an ultrasound of my abdomen to rule out malignant masses. My joints were tapped to check for fluid abnormality. A lot for a little guy to endure. I was wiped and my ankles looked funny having been shaved for the taps. I know Brown will make fun of me!

Unlike in Walpole, these people gave me a sedation reversal shot that quickly made it possible for me to head home with my full senses, not disoriented and lethargic. Thankfully, all of the results came back normal: the lone exception; slight immune-mediated arthritis in the joints. I was told that was no big deal and quite normal given my age.

Given the results, Dr. Johns and Brum thought it important for me to see a neurologist right away. Our love affair with the vet continues, Ais. We'll be back here tomorrow morning. Before long we'll be given our own VIP parking space.

Tired of being poked
and prodded,
Sull

Dear Sull,                                                                     August 16, 2012

Your true grit was on display yet again today, sweet boy.

Dr. Arendse put you through a complete battery of neurological tests and despite uncovering decreased withdrawal reflex in your bad leg, everything else checked out normal.

Dr. A spent twenty-five minutes explaining the complexity of your problem and believes an MRI and spinal tap to be the only two remaining diagnostics to truly pinpoint the root of your neurological weakness. Dr. A and I sat together on the waiting room bench, you stood at attention, watching the hustle and bustle of hospital business – saying hey to every pup that passed by.

Before confirming tomorrow's full day tests and learning the pre-procedure protocol (no food after midnight, unlimited water, yadda yadda yadda), she tenderly paused and said, "Aislynn, we have no idea what the MRI and tap will show. I am very concerned, given Sullivan's profound lameness and knuckling, that bone cancer is a strong possibility."

You know I've been Googling everything since the onset of your problem, and have certainly done my share of homework reading about bone cancer and know it to be a very viable possibility with a grave prognosis. Tears in my eyes, Dr. A reached over, resting her hand on my shoulder and said, "We just don't know. These tests will fill in the gaps and with the necessary information, we can come up with a plan."

The ride home was silent: the only sound, an intermittent snore from your weary body, sprawled comfortably on the passenger seat. To celebrate your bravery and spoil you with tasty favorites before a scary day of testing, I made a quick stop at Shaw's and bought a small rotisserie chicken and a baked potato for your dining pleasure. You gobbled up the treat, and were even gracious to share a few scraps with your brothers.

Your strength is ever-growing and resolve inspiring, while mine is weakening. In moments of despondency, I look at you – my little yellow dog from rural Tennessee, and see the strength of a giant and heart of a lion. Tomorrow won't be easy, my good friend. I will be with you every step of the way. Be strong. You are my beacon. My shining light.

Praying for answers,
Aislynn

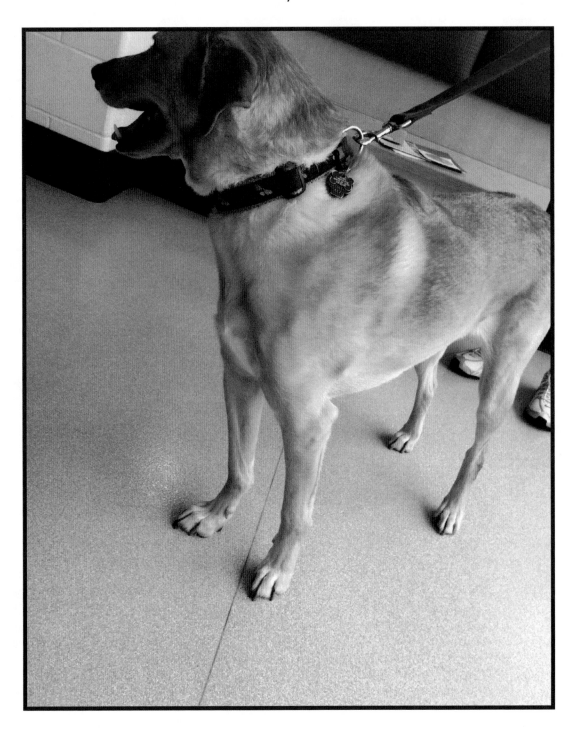

Dear Mom,

Didn't sleep well last night, tossed and turned. The butterflies that have been fluttering in my stomach with increasing frequency made a midnight appearance and left me feeling uneasy and anxious. I was leery to leave the safety of Norfolk, totally dreading another trip to Jamaica Plain. For the first time in my life I didn't want to get in the car. I stood in the backseat praying for red lights and traffic jam delays, desperately hoping to lengthen time together in the shelter and security of my big, beloved Ford Flex.

We arrived. Butterflies had butterflies and they all were boogying in my

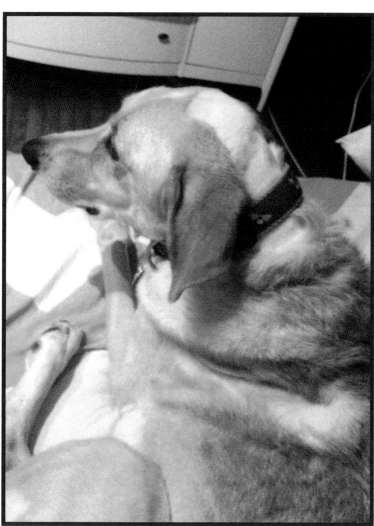

gurgling gut. Not even the mechanical door could bring a smile to my resolute face.

After a brief stint in the waiting area, a liaison called my name. She took off my bee collar and affixed a hospital admission band around my neck. We said goodbye. I was scared and could tell you were too.

I had joint taps of my left shoulder, elbow and spine; an MRI of my spine and brachial plexus; and radiographs of my left front leg. What did my future hold?

No one told me I would look like a circus freak after these tests. Mirroring a patchwork quilt, I had a 4x7 inch shave area on the top of my head, a hairless 10x6 inch rectangle above my bad leg, four 2x2 stripes around my tapped legs and the obligatory bald spot on my right ankle for the catheter. Yikes. How long is it going to take for my hair to grow? What are people going to think of me? I look so weird.

You and Dr. A talked about the findings and I was in and out, still loopy from my testing. I heard quite clearly that I was to be on a laundry list of medications including doxycycline, clindamycin, tramadol, gabapentin and prednisone. Ugh! You had better keep the chicken, potatoes, peanut butter and yummy flavored pill pockets in the camouflage queue if I'm going to have to endure this intense pill intake regimen.

Can we go home now? I miss Murphy and Brownie. I just want to sleep in my chair and be done.

Tired,
Sully

Dear Strauss,                                                      August 20, 2012

Just talked to Dr. A. Good news, bad news. No sign of cancer, but no abnormal sight of anything. Would you believe nothing major appeared on your MRI/tap to help diagnose your condition? How can this be? We have exhausted all diagnostic options! You are physically a shell of yourself with lameness intensifying by the week, but yet nothing can be identified. I am at a loss. Frustrated and Helpless. Where do we go from here?

Dr. A spotted slight irregularity in your spinal fluid which could point to an auto-immune disease such as lupus, thyroiditis, generalized demodectic mange and myasthenia gravis. She has prescribed a number of medications, which, when married together, should combat and curtail the possible infection and growing pain.

I will purchase a large pill organizer, restock on pill pockets and some of your other edible diversionary favorites, and make certain my alarm clock is set for the proper round the clock dosing times to ensure you receive your medication perfectly without error.

I am praying, Sully. Praying that this is the answer.


Oh, I need a pill cutter too…
Aislynn

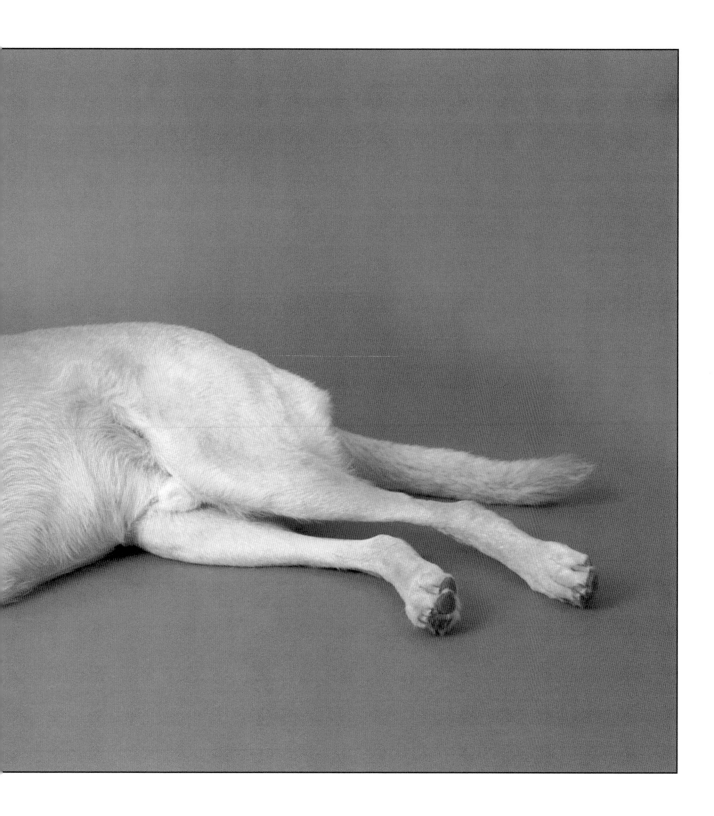

Dear Mom,                                                    September 1, 2012

I am so sorry… and wicked embarrassed.

Some of these pills are making me so thirsty that I feel the need to drink

and drink. Forgetting how much I've had, I get a compelling urge to tinkle and can't always seem to make it outside fast enough to go! I've had accidents everywhere. Sometimes in the night, I go in my sleep, and don't even know what I've done. You've had to buy pee pads and Tide detergent in bulk to keep up with my growing laundry and hygiene needs. I feel ashamed.

The pills have also amped up my appetite. I pride myself on maintaining a svelte, muscular, 58-pound physique, but my last stand on the scale had me up to 62! I'm starting to get self-conscious and want to preserve my boyish figure. Don't want to be a slow heavyweight when I am well enough to run again. No Weight Watchers for me!

The medication has bettered my mood. I find myself feeling more like

myself again. I've had more energy, have taken to many of my old likes, namely sitting in the back end of the car patrolling the neighborhood, and engaging my brothers in some light hearted play on the porch. Am I really getting better or are all these pills just covering the pain?

Despite all this, my leg isn't improving. Honestly think it may be getting worse. I've lost all muscle mass around my bone, can't walk without knuckling and can only place a small hint of weight on that leg.

I know we see Dr. A for a recheck soon. Think she'll have any new treatment suggestions? Something's gotta give. The pills aren't helping!

Tired of pills and tired of limping,
Sully

Dear Middle Bro,                                                    September 9, 2012

   We know how kind the people at Angell have been to you. Murph and I have decided to participate in the MSPCA/Angell Walk for Animals to support their cause. We've collected donations amongst our respective friend circles and have raised $650. Murphy wanted me to add that he's raised more dough, but goodness – he's three times

my age and has more contacts! Murph should be in sales. He enjoys working the crowd!

   Big Murph has committed to make the walk around the Boston Common. With weakening, arthritic hind legs, he's been going for small, training walks and swimming with Suzy Starr at Paws in Motion to beef up cardiovascular fitness and joint flexibility. He's pumped and committed. He might be the only dog wearing Easy Spirits or New Balances with inserts, but hey – not too shabby for a thirteen year old. He's quite proud of his newly defined pecs and abs. A French Poodle keeps calling him for play dates!

   Ais made red t-shirts reading Team Sullivan with a photo of you on the front. Murph and me let the creative juices flow and made bandanas that say: WALKING FOR MY BROTHER.

   Ais just told us you won't be able to come. Bummer! Your leg's gotten really bad. But ya know what bro? Next year. Next year let's do the walk the three of us, as a golden, triumphant brotherhood. I believe these good folks will be able to get you well real soon.

   I've been digging deep to curtail my rascal ways. Since Ais has been so stressed making sure you're getting all the attention you need, I've taken a hiatus from jumping, gum chewing, rock eating and counter surfing. I'm still young and mischief is my MO, but I am trying to show more self-control and obedience! With each step around the Common I'll be thinking about you.

                          I look up to you, man.
                          Brown Town

Dear Sullivan,                                                    September 21, 2012

We've had two follow up visits with Dr. A and have a tentative diagnosis, one that scares me in ways I can't even describe or comprehend. Think we will get a second opinion or maybe three or four to confirm.

Dr. A's attention to your care has been unparalleled. She has graciously accepted dozens of questioning phone calls from a tearful, confused me, and has tapped a myriad of professional resources to obtain a broader understanding of your clinical presentation.

Her diagnosis: Nerve Sheath Tumor

Her recommendation: Amputation of your left leg.

I can't even bear the thought. My heart aches.

Dr. A has assured me that pups rebound beautifully from surgery and quickly return to normal life, a better life, without pain and hindrance.

Let's get a second opinion. I will stop at nothing to get as much information and confirmation before accepting this scary procedure, especially one so radical and invasive. You have to believe I am doing all I can to do right by you.


So not the news we were hoping for... but might it be for the best?
Aislynn

Hey buddy,                                                    September 22, 2012

   While swimming laps today in the pool (the goggles you bought me for Christmas have increased my speed), Dr. Starr and Ais talked at length about your leg and ongoing Angell appointments. Dr. Starr mentioned that her husband, Dr. Knapp, formerly worked at Angell as an orthopedic surgeon.

I tried to overhear all of what was being said, but I had chlorine in my ears and was all too focused on retrieving my favorite yellow and orange sun-like disc toy to pay close attention. Cut me some slack. I admit to being a little high maintenance, I spend most days just relaxing by the stonewall, sleeping on the Tempurpedic, begging for woofies, loving my Ais and keeping you and Brownie in line that once Saturday rolls around, it's Murph time and I am one focused dude in the water. Should get my Life Guard certification next month!

Shook my head a few times releasing some water droplets, and took a short break on the wading ramp long enough to hear that Dr. Starr is inviting you and Ais over tonight to have Dr. Knapp take a quick peek at your leg.

Sounds like he really knows his stuff.

I'll ask Ais if Brown and me can come for moral support. Brotherhood Strong. And maybe an ice cream at the Black Cow after?

                    Just keep swimming,
                    Your big bro, Murph

Dear Murph Man,                                          September 22, 2012

    Thanks for the tip, dude. Dr. David Knapp was awesome. After watching me walk through the gate and feeling my leg from toenail to shoulder, without pause, he definitively said I have a nerve sheath tumor in my brachial plexus (which I learned is a fancy word for armpit). Glad I wore deodorant for the exam! Seems these types of conditions are really hard to diagnose and often

don't show up on MRIs which explains why every test has turned up empty.

    He agreed with Dr. A. My leg isn't going to get better. I'm going to have to lose it. There is no other viable treatment alternative.

    I'm so scared.

    I'm going to be a three-legged dog!

    David and Suzy rubbed my belly, even found the special spot that makes my leg twitch and causes my small orthodontia needing teeth stick out forming my signature wry smile. Somewhat shuttered and stunned by the terrifying diagnosis, I listened to Dave's reassuring words. Said my other legs are in great condition and able to bear additional weight. Unlike dogs that have been hit by cars or been hurt in other accidents, I've been able to condition my body over these last few months to walk on three legs. I'm only using my bad leg for occasional balance checks and even then, it's just my toenails that scrape the ground. Dave offered encouragement and assured me I'd come out of surgery without burden, my leg problem solved and able to live a happy, healthy life for many years.

Ais told Dave that we were going back to Angell for a second opinion with Dr. Sisson. He knows Dr. Sisson well, and trusts his medical acumen.

Thanks for hanging in the car for support. Ais promised ice cream. I'll save you a few licks from my cup. Think we can snuggle together tonight on the Tempurpedic? Your backside is one of the most comforting places I know.

Can you promise people won't make fun of me, walking on three legs and all? Will they stare? At this point I think I'll take the curiosity and looks just to be able to walk again without pain and limitation. I know you'll love and accept me unconditionally.

You'll always have my back, right!?

Sull

Not gonna bore you again with the details about the car ride to Jamaica Plain, the automated door, circumnavigating industrious cleaning people and my assessment of yet another doctor and their support staff.

Dr. Sisson confirmed the inevitable. I'm going to lose my left leg.

After Sisson's exam, I laid on the cold floor just staring upward at the big stainless light fixture. My vision became spotty given my prolonged stare, and I hypnotically zoned out of the here and now, and mentally journeyed back in time to the carefree days in the dirt holes of Miss Emily's yard, reservoir runs where three laps around wouldn't even tire my bones and three months ago when I was of full health and strength, four-legged and happy.

Throughout the exam, the doctor was very businesslike and aloof. He didn't carry savory treats in his white coat like Dr. Johns, and spent more time

typing on his computer than talking to you or petting me. Until the end of the visit.

He got down on all fours and sat, rubbing his thumb against my forehead and said "Lemme tell you a quick story." Years ago, Dr. Sisson diagnosed a cattle dog with a nerve sheath tumor and the same treatment was advised. The dog's owners were devastated thinking their beloved pup would no longer be able to herd and run through the fields given his three-legged configuration. Months after the amputation, the doctor received word that the dog had not only recovered beautifully but had resumed all herding duties with proficiency, speed and grace. Tears flooded the stoic doctor's face. He paused for a moment and wiped his eyes with his sleeve. He then lowered his head, kissed me on the nose and said, "You, my friend. You will do just fine. Soon they will say the very same things about you."

Before leaving we made an appointment to meet the surgeon.

This is all happening so fast,

Sull

Dear Sylvie, September 25, 2012

I think you missed the devastating verbal blow at today's appointment with Dr. Sisson. You appeared catatonic and detached after the physical exam, and for that I'm grateful.

The doctor mentioned that despite amputation, nerve tumors typically reappear in the remaining limbs or spinal area within one to two years. Recurrence at that time is fatal.

Grandma and I looked at each other. Stunned. Tears welled in our eyes.

I looked over at your nana. She was sitting pretzel style on the ground to your left, rubbing your back. Overcome, she burrowed her head into the nape of your neck and repeated, "No...no!" over and over in a hushed, weepy stricken whisper. A strong, stubborn Polish woman, grandma never cries. Her emotional implosion was too much to bear. I felt my lungs suffocatingly constrict, my heart rate rapidly elevate and saw an ever-growing roundel of fallen tears soak my pant leg. Remorsefully, I left the room, needing to catch my breath, wipe my eyes and regroup.

How unfair. How painful. How extreme.

How could this be happening? And why? For what purpose?

To you. The sweetest, most unassuming pup. Whose greatest life joy is running free?

Your beginnings so humble. You fought for survival on the Tennessee 40, and now again, you are faced with a difficult battle of Herculean proportion for life and mobility.

How cruel.

You've endured insensitive and inaccurate veterinary care, horrific pain, medical diagnosis ambiguity, testing galore and are now to undergo a terribly invasive and aggressive surgery that offers no true guarantee for longevity and healing. Yet through every obstacle and set back, you have and continue to display unsurpassed courage, steadfastness and fight.

Unable to move about without pain or ease, you have still entertained your brothers in play, jumped in the car for rides and tried to go on, business as usual, without complaint. You've had to consume pills like I eat M&Ms and live every day wondering, "What's going to happen to me?" Slow to trust and accept by nature, I am being forced to entrust you, one of my most treasured, beloved dears to a team of doctors who, though kind, are fallible and imperfect.

I promise you this, dear friend. Whether we have days, years or a lifetime together I vow to flood each moment with joy, gratitude and much love. Each day is a special gift to be enjoyed with expectation, good cheer, and treasured memories. Here's to carefree, sunny afternoons on the driveway blacktop, drives to who knows where, homemade yummy indulgences, nightly cuddles and reservoir runs galore. Life is going to be amply rich, one day at a time.

I need my heart to catch up to my head...

Ais

Dear Sully,                                                          September 27, 2012

It's very late. We just got home from our meeting with Dr. Casale, one of Angell's top surgeons. Our appointment was at 6:30 and we didn't end up leaving til 10:00. Her attention to detail, clear explanations and thorough physical exam was unparalleled. As a result of the significant weakness in your tricep, she wondered if perhaps you endured a mild trauma; twist or strain, which has yielded irrevocable damaging consequences. Regardless of the diagnosis, amputation is still required given the intense, irreversible nature of the muscle atrophy. That said,

Dr. Casale's diagnosis is hopeful and cautiously optimistic as it offers a counter to the scary nerve sheath tumor cancer prognosis, and perhaps even nullifies or challenges Dr. Sisson's 1-2 year maximum grim life expectancy projection.

She also insisted on a gratis set of x-rays of your hind legs to ensure strength and stability pre surgery. The test showed mild, age appropriate hip dysplasia, but nothing all too debilitating or concerning given your impending procedure.

Dr. Casale generously and kindly took the time to show me all of your imaging slides so I could understand visually what was clinically wrong with your leg. We sat together in a dark room, staring at a large computer screen chock full of white, black and grey shaded images. Dr. Casale would say, "See this? That's Sully's spine. Oh and over here is his tricep, the grey area shows the atrophy." Together we mulled over all the x-ray slides and MRI findings. Though a medical neophyte, I will forever appreciate the time and patience she offered to explain things to me as it, in some small way, offered hope, learning and context.

Like Dr. Johns, she had a pocket full of woofies. During the x-ray review you laid at her feet, patiently waiting for the small smackerels she offered you every now and again. She couldn't get over your gentleness and long suffering.

Though I am terrified for your surgery date, October 3, I don't think you could be in better, more capable hands. I have all the faith in the world in Dr. Casale. Like everyone who meets you, she fell in love with your sweet, yet tenacious spirit.

You're in with the best,
Ais

Just a few long hours before surgery.

Lots of prayers.

Lots of soul searching.

Lots of questioning.

Lots of special jaunts and favorite treats to spoil you rotten.

We went to Castle Island in South Boston for a hot dog at "Sully's" and a sit on the beach to watch the planes prepare for landing. We enjoyed long, aimless, serendipity car rides to nowhere where you were able to relax yourself completely and just enjoy the freedom of the open road. We frequented Bubbling Brook and Dairy Queen for a little vanilla ice cream goodness. I even took you on a quick, seasonably chilly spin down the Charles in the kayak. Pet Smart and Especially for Pets were near daily trips, purchasing needed and unneeded pre-surgery supplies and just because special yummies. You were spoiled with scrumptious dinners of fish, meatloaf, grilled chicken and baked potatoes; you loved every last bite.

A once solo sleeper on the puffy chair or couch of your choosing, the last few months you've taken to sleeping in bed with Murph and me. Murph has been most accommodating and willing to share space; the two of you so enjoy cuddling together. In the quiet, reflective pre-sleep moments, I hold your head in my arms and wonder – am I doing right by you? Is this what you would choose for yourself? Do you want to live the rest of your days on three legs? Are you

scared for your surgery? Do I have your permission to go forward with this? These harsh questions haunt me, keep me up at night, and worry my fragile soul.

I am struggling with reconciling and accepting the unknown. Despite having some of the top veterinary minds look at your leg, a clear, definitive consensus diagnosis has yet to be achieved.

Yes, it is thought to be trauma to the tricep or a nerve sheath tumor but we just don't know for sure. Amputating your leg when "we just don't know for sure" seems premature, perhaps even negligent and of questionable judgment. Why couldn't a color gradation have shown up on the MRI to yield a tumor? Why were the x-rays of your humerus normal when your leg is 98% lame? Intellectually, I know amputation is the best decision. It offers you a cessation from pain, and unencumbered walking. I'm just waiting on my questioning heart to support this same conclusion.

Many doubters and skeptics have questioned the lengths (time, effort, emotion and escalating costs) we have willingly expended to figure out the nature and treatment of your problem. These people are of the mindset that dogs are merely pets; whereas I believe they are true family. You have offered more unwavering support and unconditional love than I ever could deserve. You have given me your best each and every day, and in turn, I owe you the same. We made promises to each other when our story began on April 30, 2005 and I am wholeheartedly committed to upholding mine for better or worse. Despite tens of thousands of dollars in vet bills, money that could have been used to buy a dream Cape cottage, trips back and forth to Angell and the loss of self-employment billable hours to attend medical appointments – you have been worth every charge, every trip, every schedule change and every other personal purchase not made.

Others have said, "You can't have a three legged dog. He won't be able to move around normally. He'll be handicapped. That's cruel." This experience has and will continue to offer us a wonderful opportunity for teaching moments, education and perspective. Your example of resolute courage will give people reason to pause, want to learn the specifics of your long journey, smile and be in awe of your strength, bravery and dogged determination.

Tomorrow is the big day.

This experience has forced me to overcome worrisome emotional barriers. How will I be able to send you in for a series of invasive testing? How will I be able to accept the surgeon opinion and agree that amputation is the only option to ensure you a good quality of life? And now. Perhaps the scariest grouping of questions: How will I be able to drop you off for surgery knowing what you are about to endure? How will I react to seeing you, my best pal, three-legged for the first time? Will you be in pain? Will you be able to walk out of the hospital on your own? Will your tail wag in circles? What will be your recovery time? Residuals? Life Expectancy?

These questions are too much to bear. I feel as though I'm engaged in emotional and spiritual warfare. I am worried and stressed, dear friend. I know this is all for the best. Your bravery is unrivaled. I am completely inspired and in awe of your strength and courage. Your example is what has gotten me through these difficult days.

Good night.

Ais

Dear Mom,                                                    October 2, 2012

Laying on your warm, safe bed, with Murph snoring at my feet and you at my side, I feel a surreal sense of peace and calm. My belly is full from an early

dinner of fish and baked potato, and a Himalayan bone dessert chaser. But despite being surrounded by my favorite things (and Brown down the hall in his studio), I can't seem to shake my fearful nerves for tomorrow.

I see the concerned look on your face. I watch the tears intermittently fall to the pillow as you rub my ears with one hand and fidget on your iPhone with the other.

After sending your final text for the night, you sigh and tenderly kiss the middle of my head. In that moment I look at you, with weary eyes and a thankful heart, and give you the permission and authorization you've been so desperately seeking. All available options and alternatives have been exhausted. Every non-amputation remedy stone unturned. There is no turning back or second-guessing. The scheduled amputation surgery will occur. My eyes tell a

story of loyal acceptance, and reflect a profound appreciation and gratitude to you for your steadfast care and sacrificial love.

Tomorrow's the big day, Ais. Big changes in store.

I'm scared but ready,
Sully

Dear Mom,                                             October 3, 2012

Didn't sleep a wink. Your heavy breathing, Murph's occasional snore and the drone of 2 am television infomercials was the background evening hum for a sleepless, worried night. You lapsed in and out of sleep, but never stopped rubbing my ears and holding me tight.

Morning came all to soon.

The house was quiet. Even Brown's regular disorderly conduct was at a

minimum. Love was exchanged tenderly between the golden brotherhood before I hopped in the car for what was to become a life altering experience. I was leaving home on four legs, and would be returning a few days later on three.

The car ride was silent. We obtained a quick traffic report on WBZ1030 then turned off the radio. Our preoccupied minds were running a mile a minute. Our stomachs, anxious and upset.

We made the consequential right hand turn from South Huntington into the Angell driveway, which has become a home away from home over the last few months. We shared a quiet moment before heading in. Just us. You assured me I would be okay. That you wouldn't leave my side. That I would be able to run the reservoir soon. Skeptical, I had to believe you; unwavering faith had to outweigh doubt and concern. I jumped from the car and hobbled through the automated doors. A liaison was waiting and she took us into a small room. You were informed of timetables, communication channels and asked to sign some obligatory pre-surgery authorization paperwork.

Though tall in stature, today you looked diminutive. A shell of your usual confident, composed, independent self. Pale too. Vulnerable and fragile. The sleeve of your green "Feelin' Lucky" t-shirt was wet from wiping away tears, and you held tight to the desk, white knuckled, so not to pass out given your anxious wobbly legs.

The aide unclipped my embroidered collar once again and placed an orange "surgery" band around my neck in its place. It was time to say goodbye. You knelt on the ground. I nuzzled close, my head on your shoulder. You lovingly squeezed my neck, kissed the top of my head and said, "Only you have the strength and courage to go through this. I love you to the moon and back."

Drop off was early and my surgery wasn't to begin until five in the afternoon. I sat in a tall, large studio for hours. You left my red, heart-printed blanket as a comfort of home, and I rested on that. It smelled of last night's burned Black Coconut Yankee Candle and had a few lingering Himalayan bone crumbs stuck to the fuzzy fleece fibers.

I waited, and waited. Kind women dressed in blue scrubs took me outside on small jaunts to tinkle, made sure I had ample water, and even sat with me trying to comfort my worried mind. I tried to sneak a treat or two, but everyone stood fast to the rules: no woofies before surgery! Pups were coming in and out. Some were wearing the oh-so embarrassing e-collar cone of shame while others were shaved and stitched from surgical procedures. Classical music echoed from the ceiling speakers and reminded me of car rides in grandma's car. Hospital life was intriguing and held my attention in dribs and drabs, but my mind repeatedly wandered. I worried about you. Worried about the imminent pain. Worried about my recovery. Worried about life as a "tripawd". Worried about my unknown future.

A large, but gentle man came into my space mid afternoon, sat with me for a while, repositioned my blanket and gave me a little shot of something though I'm not so sure exactly what it was. I felt sleepy. I can't remember much of what happened next.

When I awoke from surgery I was in a fair amount of discomfort. Cogent enough to realize I had survived the procedure, I breathed a small sigh of thankful relief. I was reluctant to stir from my resting position, afraid to stand up and risk a stumble or fall. Though I felt phantom pains, the wound soaker alleviated much of the soreness and made me feel quite comfortable.

Hours after surgery, hospital staff came into my studio, offered me a small meal and took me outside for a bit of fresh air. Cautious, I slowly stood. Wobbly in the beginning, I acclimated myself to my new three-legged stance, balanced, and hopped down the hall to the outdoor area. The feeling was odd and unfamiliar but despite pain from the stitches, the terrible, throbbing, relentless ache I had been living with for nearly four months was gone.

Wanting to go home to see my brothers and cuddle on my favorite "Chappy Wrap", I was told I had to stay for three days to ensure proper pain management, early progressive healing, and demonstrate ever-proficient ease navigating on three legs.

I did it.

Sully

My valiant hero,                                                    October 6, 2012

Words cannot express my true admiration for you. Your courage knows no limit.

Just received the pathology report: Nerve sheath tumor, soft tissue sarcoma and mild thickening and mild atrophy of the tricep area.

Dr. Casale performed a beautiful surgery.  She was able to get one centimeter margins, reaching normal nerve area, and extracted a cluster of lymph nodes that, upon testing, were non-cancerous. Your incision is 12 inches long. Dr. Casale said this was a "great report. Couldn't be better. Got it all. This is everything we could have hoped for."

Amazing news!!

I am so eager to bring you home, but anxious and cautious just the same.

After arriving at Angell, I was given a brown paper bag filled with Tramadol, Rimadyl, Cephalexin and a discharge pamphlet with various instructions and details. I asked to see Dr. Casale. I wanted to express my profound gratitude for her perfectly executed surgery and dutiful care. She came out in full surgical regalia, reiterated the wonderful pathology news and gave me the greatest gift I could have asked for. A healthy you!

Aware of my nervous apprehension to see you three-legged for the first time, Dr. Casale sat with me on the hard, wooden bench in the Angell waiting area. Her pager was lighting up like a Christmas display but paid it no attention. She waited with me until you came out. A gesture I will never forget.

Before long, I heard the familiar jingle of your name and licensing tags as well as the clickity-clack of a three-legged pup emerging from the surgical wing. I saw you, my brave, beloved hero. Rather than coming over immediately, you paused at the pharmacy to offer a quick hello and sniff to a husky waiting for a medication refill. I shouted, "Sully!" and you darted towards me with great purpose. As you raced my way, Dr. Casale compassionately reached for my hand and said, "There's your boy!! Doing great. He's going to be just fine. Just fine. Such a sweet, special boy." I began to cry. No longer tears of sadness or fear. Tears of joy. True joy!

Tail wagging, tongue dangling from your mouth, quintessential goofy smile plastered on your face. You were happy. My Sully was back!

Our reunion was tender and sweet.

Precious moments. Precious memories.

I proudly took your leash, gave you a ginormous hug with all the TLC I could muster and said, "Let's go home!"

We left the hospital to stares, snickers, awwww's and even a few "Look at that poor dog.

He's different!"

Poor dog?

Different?

Viva la Difference!

My dog was abundantly wealthy with possessions of courage, bravery and resilience. I was rich with copious happiness and pride for my best friend was finally restored to good health! Triumph had overcome adversity and trial.

Brave and Courageous. Ready to inspire many.

Ais

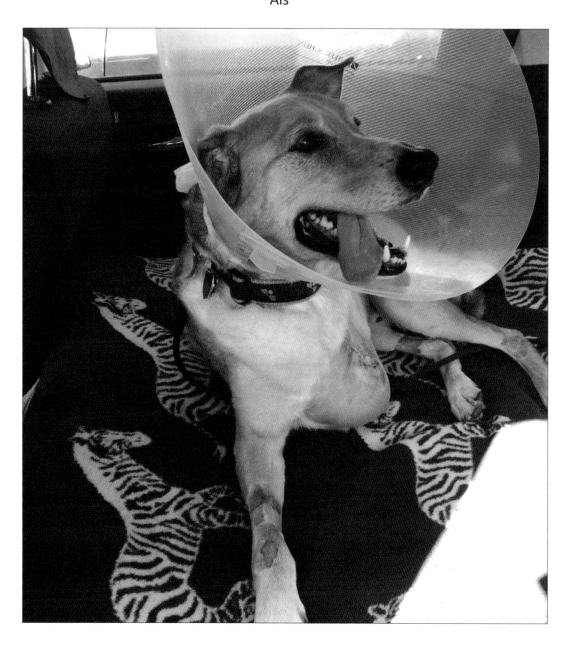

Dear Sullivan,                                                October 20, 2012

As thrilled as I was to have you home, I was equally terrified.

I called a handful of neighbors to be in the availability queue upon our October 5th arrival home to help lift you out of the car, not wanting to physically tax you, disrupt your healing incision or induce any pain. After opening the back trunk, three men positioned themselves in perfect form to lift you out. You looked them in the eye, shook off, then independently leapt from your favorite seating space onto the hard pavement. We all gasped. I shouted, "No, Sully!" No stumble. No hesitation. You hopped forward and began inquisitively sniffing the trees and grass to see what new scents had developed since your three-day yard patrol sabbatical. In that defining moment I knew. You were ready to roll.  The old Sully was back! True to form, your strength strengthened me and I knew everything was going to be okay.

The screened porch became your temporary home for a few weeks. With no stairs to navigate, and close proximity to the comforting sights and sounds of your outdoor happy haven, the porch was the perfect place to ensure a safe and speedy recovery. I made a temporary bed for

you on the futon. Large, firm and comfortable, you could fully sprawl out and relax.

Though eager to flood you with welcome home love and support, Brown and Murphy spent time upstairs, outside and on play dates with their friends so you could recover in peace and avoid any playful roughness mishaps. Young Brown enjoyed many overnights with his posse. He developed quite the curiosity and fondness for your "cone", and took to gnawing on it, trying to release you from its bondage confinement. A true partner in crime, while I am sure you appreciated his kind attempts for escape, the cone needed to stay on to prevent incision licking, infection and irritation.

We are so blessed to have an amazing network of friends and family, my friend. Flowers, meals, homemade desserts, cards, yummies from Especially for Pets and so much more delectable and loving goodness has graced our doorstep since your return home. My cell phone and Facebook page have been abuzz with messages of concern and care from friends near and far. Everyone has wanted to wish you a speedy recovery and offer healing thoughts. You are loved.

Murph went on a shopping spree and purchased, with his allowance money, your very own Tempurpedic bed. He was certain its firmness would comfortably assist as you got up and down from rest. He also chose an elevated feeding station designed to ensure balance and stability so you wouldn't need to awkwardly bend over to eat meals.

Some surgeons opt to wrap the incision site post procedure but Dr. Casale chose to keep yours open to air to facilitate healing. Cautious to not have debris or foreign matter enter the wound; we dressed you in a small, children's t-shirt. I know the "cone" and t-shirt made you feel self-conscious; but alas, the unusual combination accelerated healing and got you quickly on the mend.

Sullivan, you are always one to break the boundaries of reasonable expectations and your healing process yielded no exception. Your post surgery homeward bound leap from the car was the first indicator. You constantly pushed the envelope to test your returning dexterity and balance, and consistently exceeded every recovery timeline benchmark.

The first morning home, you went outside with grandma to tinkle, survey the yard and sniff your regular haunts. Upon coming in, you joyfully bolted up the stairs, ran into my bedroom and jumped on my bed waking me from a sound slumber. Surprised to see you, and not your mischief making younger brother, I smiled with profuse glee and gratitude. Running, jumping and stairs were all on the short list of things not to do so soon after surgery but there's no stopping you now, my courageous, remarkable tripawd super dog.


You are amazing!

Ais

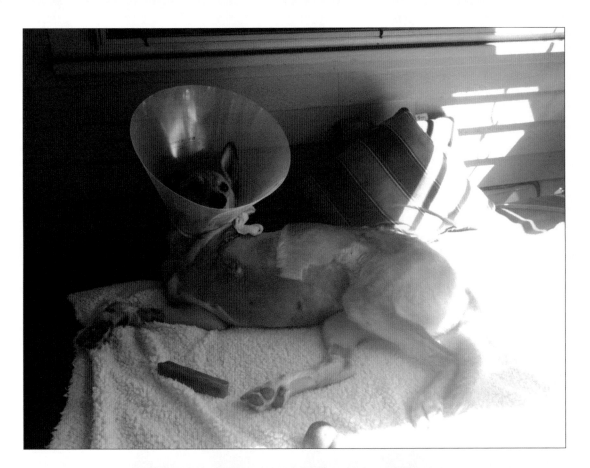

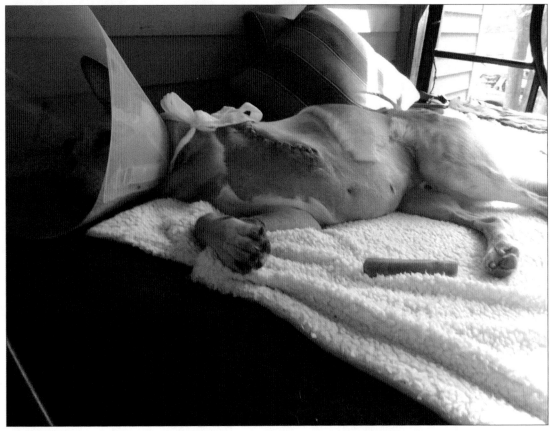

Dear Mom,                                        October 21, 2012

The day has finally come!

My excitement, uncontainable!

We are headed to the reservoir!!

I know you are nervous and apprehensive.

Afraid I will tire or stumble.

You keep telling me we will only go a quarter of the way around and to pace myself!

But I have other plans...

You watch.

Hurry! Hurry! Put on your sneakers!

Let's hit the road!!!

Happy days are here again!

I am gleeful! FINALLY!
Sully

Dear Sully,                                                October 21, 2012

    I don't think today could have been anymore beautiful. Wow! Fall in New England. Crisp air. Breathtaking foliage. Pumpkins and corn stalks on festive display at local, suburban farm stands. And you, my heroic dog, ready to return to your favorite place of bliss for the first time since the onset of your medical problem.

    I made the wide right turn onto Ash Street off of Commonwealth Avenue in Weston as you paced the backseat, whimpering ever so slightly. Your snivel crescendoed into an expectant howl as we navigated the windy road, and entered the reservoir clearing. You knew exactly where we were. Sights of familiarity: A packed parking lot filled with luxury SUV's, prep school stickers adorning many a back window, pups getting leashed to cross the busy street to then run free in a field of thistle and lavender and ducks flying low preparing to land in the lush waters of the reservoir. Happiness. Perfection.

    Anxious to have you run amongst tree roots, energetic dogs and walkers and contend with rolling hills and unleveled terrain, I had to trust. Trust that you could do it. Trust that you would offer warning signs when you were fatigued and ready to return to the car. I thought we could start slow and just walk 1/10 of the way around; not wanting to physically tax you or do damage to your progressing healing.

    Per usual, you proved me wrong. We walked at an unhurried pace. Filled with ever-growing awe and excitement, you hopped along sniffing every tree, meandering off the marked trail, making the acquaintance of fellow canine walkers, and grabbing quick drinks from the flowing streams. You led the way and would turn back periodically as if to say, "Come on slow poke, let's get moving. Catch up to me!"

    I did my best to gauge your developing stamina and offered the opportunity to turn back at the quarter mark and halfway point but you wouldn't hear of it.

You made it around the entire 2.5 mile loop. No adverse incidents. No physical ill effects.

Only eighteen days after major, life altering amputation surgery you perfectly and effortlessly navigated wooded, rocky terrain and proved to many, myself included, the measure of your robust strength and will power.

Along the way many passersby stopped for pause. Some inquired about your disability and its cause. Others whispered, "Did you see? That dog only has three legs." Many kept walking completely unaware that you were three-legged given your proficiency and grace. A few said, "Wow, you are an inspiration! Keep up the fight."

Perhaps my favorite moment came when a rather cantankerous woman said, "Oh my! How dare you bring him here with stitches? And in that condition? He is three legged." Irked, I explained that your stitches had been removed, your incision was healing beautifully and that your fur wouldn't completely grow back for a number of months. Bothered, she continued to spew negativity and ignorance until you showed her your true grit and big heart. You heard the clink of a dog's collar and chain in the distance and exerted yourself at turbo speed, making a mad dash to see who was headed your way. The woman looked at me with surprised eyes and said, "Wow. Guess he showed me."

You've proven your courage and recovery to the masses, Sully. Your resiliency knows no limit. You have rightfully earned the respect and admiration of many, to even include the stubborn skeptics and naysayers.

I know you will likely trip, stumble or become fatigued on future walks. Though I'll likely resort to my helicopter hovering and protecting tendencies and want to coddle you; I need to respect your independent toughness and pride. Believe that you will be okay. Your body will tell us if aggravation or new problems emerge. For now, however, you are the picture of health.

You are an example of courage and I admire you more than you know.

Ais

Dear Mom,                                                      November 1, 2012

The weather is changing. Winter's chill is in the air.

We've been exploring all the local pet stores looking for a coat to properly cover my left leg area, but not hinder ambulation. Though the incision has healed well, my fur is taking a while to grow back given the post-surgery wound

soaker and medication. The cold permeates that sensitive hairless area and leaves me chilly on fall days. None of the coats fit just right. Most of them are tight, rub under my arm and cause chaffing discomfort.

Jeannine Hammond of JJ Boxer Dog Jackets kindly offered to make me my very own custom jacket. She took careful measurements of my body to ensure best fit and widened the regular Velcro strapping to prevent shifting when I run and hop about. The coat also sports a turtleneck-like feature whereby the collar can be fully extended to keep my neck and ears toasty, or rolled down to stay cool on warmer days. I gave her creative license to design a hip and trendy looking coat that hot chicks would dig, and she totally nailed it. Red is my favorite color!! The coat is accented with miniature black and white bones and has a custom big red bone on my back with my name, SULLY, inscribed.

We are preparing for the November 10th Angell/MSPCA "Run Fur Fun" 5K road race in a few days. A great time to make new friends, renew old friendships and share my eventful journey experiences of the past several months with well-wishers. I cannot wait to show off my brand new coat at the event. Should be a great day!

I know I'll turn heads! Don't forget to bring a lot of film!
Sullivan

Dear Sully,                                                November 10, 2012

TEAM SULLIVAN!!

Thirty of your closest friends joined us at Artesani Park in Brighton this morning for the "Run Fur Fun". Sporting bright red "I Run for Sullivan" t-shirts and grey wristbands, we were ready to take on the 3.1-mile course along the Charles River.

Our group won the award for "Best Team", hands down displaying the most creativity and enthusiasm. You quickly became the overwhelming fan favorite. You were the unofficial mascot of the race. Everyone wanted to give you some love, commend you for your heroic display of courage, get their picture taken with the celebrity and even seek a paw print autograph.

Participants were awe-inspired that you were able to complete the race having lost your leg just five weeks prior. What stamina! What heart!

You turned heads in your special coat! Is the rumor true you got seven marriage proposals? Is a formalized Fan Club and Facebook page now in the queue?

Many of the Angell staff and doctors who tended to you along your challenging journey were present as volunteers and were filled with great delight and satisfaction to see you doing so well.

Go Team Sullivan!

Ais

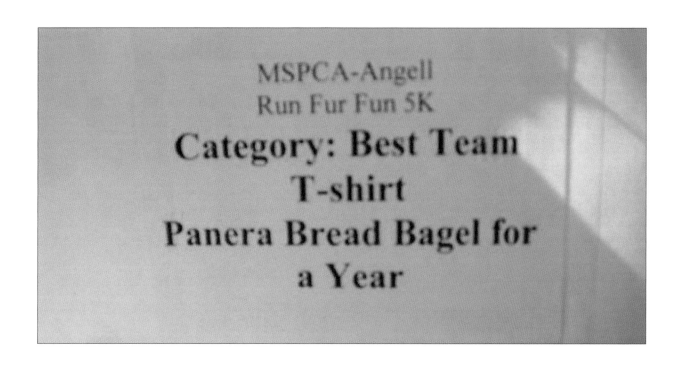

MSPCA-Angell
Run Fur Fun 5K
**Category: Best Team
T-shirt
Panera Bread Bagel for
a Year**

This time when I learned we were headed to Jamaica Plain, my paws didn't sweat and my stomach didn't anxiously tumble.

Today was a day of gratitude and appreciation - an opportunity to say thank you to the kind people who contributed to my miraculous recovery.

As I ambled through the familiar automated double doors and took a seat on the cold, clean floor of the Angell waiting area, my mind raced back in time and recounted all the trials and triumphs I had been through. I truly feel blessed to once again be able bodied, healthy, strong and happy.

Peaches & Herb were on to something with their description of reunions. But this one wasn't just good. It was amazing!

Dr. Casale and Dr. Arendse came out of the examination area together. Surprised to see me they exclaimed, "Sullivan!!!!" With broad smiles on their faces, they knelt to the floor in tandem and loved on me like crazy!

Bearing gifts, I brought both doctors a "Chappy Wrap", my favorite blanket that offered me great comfort during the long, exhaustive and emotional days of uncertainty, doubt and tough decision making. Aware of the demanding rigor of their work, I thought it appropriate for them to have a tangible object to wrap up in at night. A lasting reminder of all the love and appreciation us two, three and four legged critters have for their kindness, expertise, diligence and good judgment. Aware that many life or death result endings are sadly not as happy as mine, it is of great importance that they know how truly indebted and blessed I am for saving my life. They are truly my angels.

Smiles, laughter, tears and hugs made this reunion one for the history books. Nana snapped photos. Thanks for stopping on the way home to get a jumbo sized photo album. I keep this photo close by my bedside table for it reminds me of all that is good in this world: kindness, compassion and tender loving care.

Today was a very special day,

Sull

Dear Sullivan,                                November 14, 2012

It was so good to see you today!

You look amazing!! What a recovery!

We are both so happy to see how well you are doing, though we aren't surprised.

There's something special about you, Sullivan. You are tough and have a "can do, don't ever give up" drive that propels you forward without limit. You have an insatiable appetite for life.

You were always a trooper at your medical appointments despite being in horrific pain and not feeling well. You never complained and never fussed. You were grateful for the medical attention we were providing, and always compliant to all types of treatment.

A doctors' dream.

The technician staff always jockeyed for the opportunity to take you out during your surgical stay. You were so gentle, self-effacing, loving and brave.

Thank you for our lovely gifts. The blankets are as warm as your sweet personality.

We will both hold your story close in our hearts as it is one of survival, determination and courage. Maybe you should write a book?!

What a wonderful surprise. Please come visit again soon!

With Love,
Your Doctors

I think it's awesome that you are back in the saddle at the reservoir.

Really wasn't the same without you for a few months.

You were always the leader. You set the pace, blazed the trail and checked out the approaching four-leggeds for friendliness, weeding out the riff raff and unsociable before they came my way. You were my trusty sentinel. I never had to worry.

Unfortunately, Murph's been out of commission on the DL the last few months. His geriatric hind legs have been giving him some trouble and the big loop is too much for his arthritic gait to maneuver. I've been rolling solo or with my best Golden Retriever friend, and surrogate brother, Bodhi. As you know, Bodhi isn't all that accustomed to off-leash runs. His mom sends her golden canine on reservoir jaunts looking dapper, always perfectly quaffed and blown out, blonde curls dancing perfectly along his back. Though she signs the perfunctory permission slip for a day of fun, it's the unspoken understanding and agreement that Bodhi steer clear from the tempting mud hollows, not go beyond waist deep in the watering holes and not tangle with questionable canine bullies.

A member of the golden brotherhood, you've taught me the importance of loyalty. Certainly not a bruiser or nun chuck wielding mean junkyard dog, I simply know the importance of allegiance and take my job of protector (some would even say muscle!) very seriously. Many misjudge my naughty ways given my unassuming, affable, small boned yellow Labrador exterior but inside, I espouse a 'take no prisoner' mentality. Do not provoke, antagonize or threaten! No one messes with my posse!

When shady or menacing dogs approach, I get low to the ground, trying to assess the potential danger situation from afar. When the moment is right and I'm confident Bodhi is safe behind, I charge, growling ever so slightly to throw the challenger off guard. I make the initial introduction and do a preliminary friend or foe personality check, and nod my bestie on if the coast is clear and safe.

I have assumed the role of watchman, protector and defender in your absence.

Now that you are back in the pack I am very quick to keep a watchful eye out for you too. If dogs approach too aggressively, or inappropriately sniff you in a way or place I don't think is cool I take them out. Not viciously. I just benevolently create a diversion, engage in a little scuffle, and give you a chance to get ahead of the scallywags and retreat to safety. You've taught me well bro.

Ais isn't too keen on this confrontational behavior and often threatens to leash me. I hear her telling fellow walkers that I'm demonstrating loyalty and protection. Some think it's endearing; others are offended and frightened.

I'm devoted and have the backs of those I love. I learned that from you and I am honored to now protect you and keep you safe.

Brown Town, the Enforcer

Dear Mom,                                            December 25, 2012

Merry Christmas!

I have so much to be grateful for this holiday season.

Working the crowd, hoping to manipulate a kind soul into sharing a 'pig in a blanket' or mushroom cap at the annual Christmas party, I overheard you talking to a group of friends about changes in my disposition and personality.

"Always a sweet and gentle soul, he used to be so independent and aloof. Now he is incredibly loving, clingy and dare I say… cuddly!"

My trials and tribulations have opened my eyes to see what is truly important and lasting in life.

Tennessee living survival conditioned me to be self-reliant, slow to trust and even a little standoffish so as to not let down my guard or defenses. Though flooded with love, warmth and safety in Norfolk, early-developed cautious and protective tendencies run deep. Who said, "You can't teach an old dog new tricks?"

It wasn't until I feared losing it all that I willingly and consciously opened myself up, becoming vulnerable and exposed. Though risky, the benefits have been grand.

Be it late night cuddles in bed, sitting on the couch with my head resting on your knee, staying downstairs to listen to the laughter and banter on game nights rather than retreating upstairs to rest alone on the foot of the bed or relaxing in the family room with you in front of the fireplace; time spent together is a true gift and great blessing. I have learned to trust you explicitly and never take for granted the opportunity to have Murphy and Brown as my best buds and playmate companions. We truly are a family, kindred spirits, bound together by love.

Don't need a wrapped present under the tree this year. I received the greatest gift this fall when I regained the ability to run free!

                                        Merry Christmas,
                                        Sullivan

Dear Mom,                                    April 20, 2013

You just uttered some of my favorite words.

"Sully, wanna go in the kayak?"

I got up as fast as I could and darted to the front door. I hopped about in the driveway while you secured the big orange kayak on the roof rack and packed the car with the paddle, sunglasses, water, woofies and of course our life jackets.

So excited, I couldn't help but wonder how my three-legged stance would work in the kayak. Would I be able to balance myself without throwing off the steadiness of the boat? What if my right leg gets tired and doesn't have the stamina to hold me up during the duration of the ride? What if my unsteadiness makes the boat tip? Will I be able to swim with three legs?

Though these questions festered in my mind, I was so excited to be in the car, headed to my favorite watering hole to be preoccupied with such 'what if' concerns.

You tightened my yellow life vest and velcroed it snug around my neck for safekeeping. I sat close and secure between your legs. Your knees buttressed my haunches for safety. As we glided away from the rocky shore, I felt myself wobbling from side to side, trembling ever so slightly. I was soon able to acquire my sea legs, stabilized, and quickly got the feel for the water.

It was amazing.

Peaceful and serene.

I sat at attention for a good portion of the outing but needed to rest halfway. I was able to lie down at your feet, my head positioned on the top of the boat. So comfortable! I watched the ripples come off of the paddle and felt a few droplets of water drip on my head. It was a pleasure spending the afternoon amongst nature's beauty: baby snapping turtles, fish, fellow boaters, chirping birds and the constant hum of cicada bugs.

What fun. My fears have been allayed. I'm back in the boat again!

Can't wait for an amazing spring and
summer on the water,
Sullivan

Dar Mom,                                                                    May 2, 2013

Ugh! Today was just one of those days.

I'm feeling discouraged and depressed.

I was looking forward to trying out the new trail in Dover you've been talking about. Apparently if we follow the right markings (could be difficult for us given our directional challenges!) we can hike to Noanet Peak to see amazing views of the Boston skyline.

We were unsure of where to enter to find the trails and wandered aimlessly in circles for what seemed like an eternity. Once we found the marked trail area, we struggled to stay on course. Wanting to stay on the red trail, we lost

our bearings and wound up on the hilly, rocky terrain of the yellow path. It took all my focus and stamina to navigate the difficult, rooted, pebbly ground. I grew fatigued and needed to rest in regular intervals. You offered me water, but that didn't do the trick. I was just wiped. The combination of new turf, not knowing the ropes and having to carefully maneuver the unfamiliar trail was just too much.

On the way back we ran into a small, inviting pond and in a fit of spontaneous enthusiasm I darted into the water. Going just a little too deep I panicked and flailed my three legs to try to keep my head afloat. Brown circled, splashing his front paws as if to give me aid. You then tossed your cell phone into a small leaf pile and heroically ran into the water fully clothed to save me.

It was so embarrassing.

A harsh and sobering wake up call.

In that frenzied moment I realized the extent to which I am still physically compromised with stamina and strength limitations, never to fully regain my pre-surgery health and wellbeing. Until now, in normal, comfortable and familiar surroundings, I have been able to hang, be a competitive player and not be hindered. But here, in a new place with a tough and long footpath and enticing swimming opportunity, reality hit hard and clear.

I have never before thought of myself as disabled. I've adopted the mentality that I am more than able. While positivity and hope will continue to anchor my mind frame, today was a ground zero dose of reality. Ups and downs will come and go. I must learn and accept my limitations.

In the words of Nemo, "Just keep swimming."
Sylvie

My dear boys,                                                                May 27, 2013

Today was a day I will never forget!

Memorial Day, 2013. A day for the record books.

Perfect weather. 60 degrees and not an ounce of humidity.

Murph, you've been hanging back on reservoir trips lately because the warm, muggy weather makes it tough on your aging, tender, arthritic limbs, but today, everything was in perfect alignment and you were able to come along for the merry family outing. I know the reservoir is your happy place!

Having my three guys, together and happy, means the absolute world to me.

Many photos were taken to remember this special day.

Perfection.

The happiest family!

So blessed.


Happy day,
Ais

Dear Sully,                                                    July 12, 2013

You know I've been closely following the comings and goings of Ray Charles, the blind Golden Retriever, who has recently become an Internet sensation. Ray was born blind, and after extensive testing at Angell, it was determined that though his eyes are healthy there is a synapse disconnect between his brain and eyes making it impossible for him to see. Andrew Fales adopted Ray and gave him the opportunity for a healthy, happy life!

I received word that Ray would be "throwing out" the first pitch at the Bark in the Park event at the Lowell Spinners Baseball Game. Dogs were invited to the ballpark for a pregame parade around the field, to watch the game and enjoy special treats! Representatives from local animal shelters were also on hand to try to adopt newly rescued pups. Determined to meet Ray Charles and give you and Brown the good opportunity to meet some Spinner's players, we packed into the BMW and headed to Lowell for a nice Sunday afternoon activity. Play Ball!

There were nearly fifty other dogs and their people ready to participate in the pre-game parade. We took our place in the middle of the pack and started walking the warning track as the parade began.

Grandma was walking with you; Brown was by my side. The song "Who Let the Dogs Out" started blaring on the stadium loud speaker and you felt inspired. You high tailed it and started hopping with boundless enthusiasm, passing many of your canine parade mates. As we made the slight turn towards first base, you were leading the pack with a near 20-yard gap between the plump wheezing Beagle jockeying for second place.

Spectators were aghast and abuzz. "That dog has three legs!", "He's leading the pack", "Wow. Look at him go!", "That's so cool!". As we rounded first base, onlookers stood, inspired. You received a standing ovation and roaring cheer for your speed and uniqueness.

Brown and I raced from the back of the pack to catch up. Goosebumps and a warm feeling of pride filled my body as I scanned the crowd of people, standing in appreciation, applauding you, my hero.

After the parade we scrambled to locate Ray Charles! We found him on the main concourse and had a nice chat with his dad, Andrew and grandma, Cathy and took a few pictures.

Then, the most amazing thing happened. You sat like a gentleman to meet Ray Charles as he approached to make your acquaintance. Though blind, he stood, with an air of intrigue and compassion, inquisitively sniffing your amputation site. You two stood in solidarity: Ray, wearing his "Blind Dog" vest and you, three-legged, regaled in a green soft cast to heal a skin irritation; silently accepting and appreciating each other's differences and commonalities!

All of humanity should have witnessed today's teachable events.

Life lessons abound.

To see my hero take a figurative, symbolic victory lap around the Spinner field; having endured and overcome a traumatic year of adversity, pain and loss is reason alone to pause and celebrate. Three-legged, magnificently hopping with purposeful confidence, pride and speed to the roaring cheers of an adorning crowd, you literally and figuratively won this race and more importantly, the race of life. You are a true champion. You have overcome!

Ray's blind, intuitive awareness of your handicap and your excitement to meet a gorgeous Golden, unaware of his vision impairment is a lesson to all about unconditional acceptance and blind love.

Today was awesome!

Couldn't be prouder to call you mine!

Ais

Dear Katie,                                                                July 29, 2013

Remember that bet we made way back when?

Well, it's come to fruition!

Sully, your dog Harry and Brownie just had the most phenomenal romp around the Wheelock School fields in Medfield.

Happy as clams, the three boys engaged in a proverbial game of tag, darting in and out of the lavender fields trying to chase each other and not be last. Panting pink tongues and blonde tail tips wagging through the tall grass, the only trail of canine frolic.

In the tall grass, Sully looked as if he had all four legs.

He kept up with the group and ran with reckless abandon.

The smile on his face at the end of the walk told a story of unbridled joy and happiness, one that made the long trips to Angell, many sleepless nights and constant worry all worthwhile.


Today I am so happy!

Ais

Dear Sullivan,                                                    August 17, 2013

The word tribute is defined as a gift, testimonial, compliment or the like given as due or in acknowledgement of gratitude. My letters are a tribute: A tribute to your heroism, courage, perseverance, resilience and survivability. A tribute to the medical team whose wise council was clinically sound and compassionately rich. A tribute to friends and strangers alike that supported, prayed, affirmed and championed your journey without judgment. A tribute and celebration of the intimate and special bond between dog and human, one that is laced with unconditional love, understanding and mutual admiration.

Grateful, our story is ongoing. We will share many more car rides, wooded walks, nighttime cuddles, ice cream cones and good times.

Your dogma is affirmation-based. A creed of courage, bravery, perseverance, appreciation, steadfastness and positivity. You truly put the CAN in the word canine!

With you as my unwavering guide, I have grown leaps and bounds on this year-long journey. I have been pushed out of my comfort zone and forced to face challenges I otherwise would have deflected, ignored or cowered from.

Whenever I think I have been defeated, convinced I cannot accomplish a goal, I look down with encouragement and hope at my "Team Sullivan" wristband and visualize you, my three-legged, happy boy and think…you can do it. You can do anything. Never ever give up! You have taught me the true meaning of dogged determination.

A year ago today you could barely walk. Lame and in incredible pain you were relegated life as a passive observer. Today, you and I woke early and went for a 5am hike in Noanet Woodlands. We followed the yellow marker dots along a steep, rocky trail. You sprinted in and out of the marked path and bounded with reckless enthusiasm, while I huffed and puffed and paused from time to time to give my thighs and calves a rest from the taxing upward climb. Before long we made it to the trail peak. You stood, three-legged and confident atop a rocky landscape. The

Boston skyline to your left and a sea of breathtaking tree summits to the right. After a year of adversity and uncertainty, a true uphill battle, you have come out victorious. You are now overlooking a vista of opportunity, hope, new beginnings, pride and celebration. How exciting!

What a difference a year makes.

Who would have thought, nearly eight years ago when I met you, my emaciated, untrained yellow dog, in a Plainfield, CT highway parking lot, that your life would forever impact mine. That you would become my hero, dear friend, teacher and spiritual guide.

I thought I was saving you on April 30, 2005. Truth be told, you saved me.

Love you to the moon and back,

Ais

A postscript:

On Saturday, September 8, 2012, we gathered at the Boston Common to participate in the annual MSPCA Walk for Animals. As you recall, Sullivan was unable to participate in last year's activities given his debilitating medical condition. Running late, per usual, we hustled and found a place at the back of the long line amidst people and dogs of all shapes and sizes. Young Brown tagged along for the day and was thrilled to have his brother for company after last year's no-show.

We stood idle for what seemed like forever then slowly began to move from our place. The pace was slow at first as participants shuffled to establish a comfortable gait but before long the crowd began to disperse. Once Sullivan hit his step, our stride quickened. We passed Basset Hounds and Pugs to our left, Golden Retrievers and Min Pin's to our right. Excited by the sights and sounds of Boston's metropolis and the many canine kindred friends about, Sullivan's pace ever-increased. I found myself jogging, sometimes running to keep up with him. Brown got left in the dust, stamina waning. Huffing and puffing and requiring an Albuterol inhaler for respiratory assistance, he hung back in the middle of the pack allowing Sullivan to singly blaze the route with the frontrunners. Half way around the Common we completely separated from the masses and jogged at our own swift pace. I too could have used assistance from Brown's breathing device, but tried to maintain strength so not to hinder Sullivan's zeal.

Tourists, lookers and homeless strays smiled, gazing in awe at my three-legged pal as he hastened the route; pink tongue dangling, wry grin beaming. As we came upon the final turn, kiddy corner from the glorious State House, Sullivan had the race starters in his sights. After lapping well over a thousand two, three and four legged participants we finally made it to the head of the line.

We noticed a familiar looking soul pushing a small four-wheeled cart with two tiny dogs in tow. After a quick thought, I identified the gentleman as Carlos Arredondo, the "Cowboy-hatted" hero of the Boston Marathon bombing. Carlos selflessly and bravely ran into

Boylston Street crowd after the explosions and heroically rescued many race spectators, namely Jeff Bauman. Carlos, his wife and their two small dogs (who were pushed in a cart given their small size) were the leaders of the race in recognition of his heroic "Boston Strong" bravery.

Sully and I jogged up to the front of the pack. Mindful to give Carlos and his brood space and the opportunity to finish first we hung back a little, but engaged he and his wife in conversation. They both marveled at Sullivan's speed and were quite fascinated and inspired by his story of survival and grit. I proudly shared how the good people at Angell saved his life and that it was our good pleasure to participate in this year's walk out of appreciation for their wonderful veterinary service and compassionate, outstanding care.

At that moment, Carlos's wife turned to her husband and whispered a little something. She then looked in our direction and said, "You, Sullivan, are the real hero here. You deserve to finish first." With tears in my eyes and gratitude in my heart, I offered great thanks for their kindness but reiterated how Carlos was the ultimate hero and needed to cross first.

As we approached the endpoint, Sully and I carefully gauged our steps to ensure a first place finish to the Arredondo family. With just a few feet to go, they stopped, allowing us to finish first.

A year after life altering surgery, my little Sullivan has won the proverbial race. Alive, well, happy and swift, he lapped hundreds of dogs in a march around the Common; but more importantly, he surpassed all medical odds and has come out the true victor in life. What a difference a year makes. Here's to you, Sullivan!

## About the Author:

Aislynn Rodeghiero resides in Norfolk, Massachusetts with her three yellow dogs: Murphy (13), Sullivan (8) and Brown (3). She graduated from Boston College in 2003 and later received Master of Education (M.Ed) and Master of Social Work (MSW) degrees from Boston College and Boston University, respectfully. Aislynn has a private clinical social work practice working primarily with children impacted by familial divorce, grief and education-based challenges. A certified life coach, Aislynn employs creative therapeutic strategies to guide her clients through major life changes in a humanistic, holistic way. Aislynn is an avid basketball player and loves fall in New England.

Made in the USA
Lexington, KY
25 February 2014